The Lie of
"Christian"
Rock And Roll

Spencer Smith

Call Calling Evil Good

The Lie of "Christian" Rock and Roll

Copyright © 2016 by Spencer Smith

Note to Reader: We have done everything we can to do as thorough a job of proofreading the text and notes as we possibly can. The reader of this book should realize that this book is a first edition and first editions are notorious for overlooked errors. We want the reader to be sure that any incorrect references, deviations from the King James text, misspellings, and grammatical errors are not intentional. Errors found in quotes have been intentionally left alone for the sake of accurately telling what someone has published. If you find something that is incorrect, please feel free to bring it to our attention. We will make the necessary corrections.

DEDICATION

I would like to dedicate this book to those who were bold enough to speak out about this subject when I was a new convert. You convinced me that the Church should not be a cheap imitation of the world. Thank you.

ACKNOWLEDGEMENTS

I would like to express my gratitude to Maria Jordan, Alicia Sanders, Tonie Weddle, and Selene Mack, and Brandi Jordan for proofreading for me. Thank you so much for helping a C student from north Georgia write this book. I would also like to thank Pastor Luchon and Steve Luchon for the opportunity to have this book printed with Hilltop Publications.

TABLE OF CONTENTS

FOREWORD

I do not try to predict the future, but in this case, I can. You are going to either love or hate the subject matter of this book. Either way you will have to know that the young man who has poured his heart into not only the writing of the book but the researching of the matter as well.

Often you find young men trying to act the expert without the benefit of expertise. Spencer Smith has done his due diligence to produce a factual and compassionate treatise on the matter of the lie of "Christian Rock."

Please, take the message contained in this book to heart and put as much care and prayer into your reading as Brother Smith has put into the work before you.

Thank you for reading and may God bless you for it.

Dr. Gary Biggs
Pastor of Landmark Baptist Church
Petoskey, Michigan

"I believe that one reason why the church of God at this present moment has so little influence over the world is because the world has so much influence over the church." - Charles Haddon Spurgeon

"When the church affects the world, you have revival. When the world affects the church, you have apostasy." - Dr. Bob Jones Sr.

"When amusement is necessary to get people to listen to the gospel, there will be failure. This is not the method of Christ. To form an organization and provide all kinds of entertainment for young people, in order that they may come to the Bible classes, is to be foredoomed to failure." - G Campbell Morgan

"Modern Christians hope to save the world by being like it. But it will never work. The church's power over the world springs out of her unlikeness to it. Never from her integration into it." - A.W. Tozer

"One compromise here, another there, and soon enough the so-called Christian and the man in the world look the same." A.W. Tozer

"A whole new generation of Christians has come up believing that it is possible to accept Christ without forsaking the world." - A.W. Tozer

"There is a glorified man on the right hand of the majesty in Heaven faithfully representing us there. We are left for a season among men; let us faithfully represent Him here." - A.W. Tozer

"The Holy Spirit never enters a man and then lets him live like the world. You can be sure of that." -A.W. Tozer

"A church fed on excitement is no new testament church at all. The desire for surface stimulation is a sure mark of the fallen nature, the very thing Christ died to deliver us from." - A.W. Tozer

"We cannot afford to let down our Christian standards just to hold the interest of people who want to go to Hell and still belong to a church." - A.W. Tozer

"I'm a singer, not a preacher, I'm not looking to convert anybody." - Amy Grant, (Los Angeles Times 5/4/84)

"I'm not going to say too often that I like a cold beer while watching a football game. That might bother some of my fans." -Amy Grant, (Greensville News, 5/4/84)

"I'm trying to look sexy to sell a record..." - Amy Grant (Rolling Stone, June 6, 1985 p.10)

"Ugh! Can't you see you're not making Christianity better, you're just making Rock and Roll worse!" - Hank Hill, King of the Hill (Season 8 Episode 2: Reborn to Be Wild)

"The things that make us different, make us necessary." - Brian Jackson

INTRODUCTION

My heart is burdened for many people that are involved in the "Christian Rock" world. I fear that there are many in this group that genuinely want to reach people but are using means and methods that are destructive to the cause of Christ. Also, I'm afraid that there are many in the "Contemporary Christian World" who because of the watered-down message have never truly been born again.

I grew up in the metro Atlanta area. My family never went to church, though many would consider Georgia to be a part of the "Bible Belt." Most of the people that I grew up with were involved with some kind of church. On occasion, I was invited to a youth activity at one of these churches.

One time I was invited to attend a "Christian Rave." When I arrived, we entered a completely dark gym filled with black lights, fog machines, loud music, and dancing. The Bible was not preached, but the music occasionally made a vague reference to "God" or "Lord."

On another occasion, I was invited to a crusade at a public park. The event contained a bouncy house, hot dogs, a dunking booth, a short devotion about "God wants you to have fun," and a third-rate rock concert performed by a group of teenagers from the church. This music was woefully substandard in quality and contained few vague references to "God" and "Father."

I am still friends with the people that attended churches that held events like this. They were always cordial to me and I hold no ill will toward them whatsoever, but the question has to be asked: Why did these "Christian Rock" concerts not bring me to Christ?

I was saved at the age of 18 when a youth pastor and song leader witnessed to me about my need for Christ. My life was radically changed forever and I literally became a "new creature" (2 Corinthians 5:17). Months after my conversion, I looked back at all the religious events that I had attended as a teenager and I wondered why they did not result in my conversion. Why didn't the "Jars of Clay" album, the "Christian Rave" party, and the "Christian Rock" concert not bring me to Christ? The conclusion that I have come to, is that much of the "Contemporary Christian" movement has watered down the Gospel so much that the message is no longer being presented.

The purpose of this book is not to argue subjective music elements like that of a 2/4 beat emphasis, denominational traditions, or the use of means to evangelize the lost, but to show you that many churches are using unholy, lewd, and wicked means with the intention of achieving a holy, virtuous, and righteous end. Not only is this a logical fallacy, but it is counterproductive to the cause of Christ.

Many have heard the cliché, "The end justify the means." The problem with this philosophy is that the means DETERMINE the end. If the goal is to get the whole world to Christ, then what means do we use to accomplish this goal? Do we use the means of Gospel preaching missionaries to reach the world? Do we use the means of Gospel literature to reach the world? Or do we find out what the lost world likes (Rock and Roll) and decide to imitate that (Christian Rock) in order to reach them for Christ? Do we use flesh to make people spiritual?

How do you reach a man that loves sin? Do you use sin to reach him? How to you reach a drunk? Do you become drunk with him? How do you reach a Harlot? Do you commit adultery with her to reach her? How do you reach a violent criminal? Do you become a violent criminal to reach him? How do you reach a man that likes sex, drugs, and rock and roll? Do you use sex, drugs, and rock and roll to reach him? Did the people rescuing survivors of the Titanic get into the icy cold water with the victims so they could share common ground before pulling them from their icy demise, or did they stay dry in the boat as they did their work?

There have been those who have taken this philosophy to the extreme and have caused great reproach to come upon the name of Christ. During my years living in Tennessee, there was a preacher that wanted to reach alcoholics for Christ. Rather than invite them to church for preaching, he invited them to a special church service in which beer and liquor would be served free of charge. He wanted to use the beer to get them to church, then he wanted to preach to them about how they could be "drunk with the Holy Ghost by receiving the Holy Ghost." The service was a total disaster, resulting in zero conversions. The trustees of the church fired the pastor a few days later. I'm glad that this man is out of the ministry today.

When dealing with subjects like this, we must raise certain questions. When Christ was dealing with the woman at the well in John 4, did he become an adulterer so He could reach her? When Phillip was dealing with the Ethiopian Eunuch in Acts 8, did he become a Eunuch to reach him? When Peter preached on the day of Pentecost, did he send teams out to poll the crowd to find out what type of music they liked and then write a song with Christian words to get the message to these people? Many would say that the above sentences are absurd, but this is the logic used by many in the "Contemporary Christian" world.

When a church decides to use the world's means to reach the world, it heads down a path from which often there is no return. At the end of this path we find that the church did not convert the world, but rather the world has converted the church. The rescue workers are diving into the icy waters of the north Atlantic and nobody is left in the life boat.

My prayer is that those who would read this book are challenged to search their heart. Are you really saved? Have you been made a new creature in Christ? If so, do you see that our God is Holy and that we are His ambassadors on this earth? How can we properly present our Holy God (Isaiah 6:3)

8

when we are using unholy means?

There are Satanic forces at work today that are meant to blur the line between holy and unholy, clean and unclean, and acceptable and abominable. These lines result in the world becoming "churchy" and the church becoming worldly. When the church becomes just like the lost world that they are trying to reach, they lose all credibility. When the church loses all credibility, then men die in their sin without a true witness of the life changing power of the Gospel of Christ. Thus, the goal of Satan is accomplished.

May God speak to your heart.

WHERE DID THIS ALL BEGIN?

In order to understand the history of contemporary Christian music, one must have a basic historical and spiritual understanding of the origin of rock and roll.

It is generally believed that the first African slave ship to come to America was to the Puritan Colony of Jamestown, Virginia in 1619. The origin of much of the slave market is generally believed to be from Senegambia and the Windward Coast, known today as Senegal and The Gambia, West Africa. The last known slave ship to bring African slaves to America was the Clotilda, arriving at Mobile Bay, Alabama, in autumn 1859. It is generally believed that 12.5 million slaves were shipped to the New World, but only 10.7 million survived the trip.

The religion of the 10.7 million to come to the New World was heathenism. Cliff Odle wrote in his article: "African American Religion in Early America":

"African slaves were stolen from their homelands, and often had very little in common with each other. They spoke different languages, had different customs and prayed to different gods. Many tribes and peoples acknowledged a powerful, distant god along with lesser gods. Worshippers used many of these lesser gods as messengers to the one great god. These spirits could take the form of objects of nature like rocks, trees, or the wind. They could also take the form of tribal ancestors. They asked of

these spirits all types of blessing and favors, from good harvests and plentiful hunting to victory in tribal warfare.

The first slaves struggled to keep these old beliefs while facing new terrors. As their numbers grew, slave rebellions became an increasing concern for slave owners. In order to control the slave populations, African languages and religions were replaced with those of their masters. Puritan colonists, fearing these "heathen" people, began to baptize their slaves by the1660's. The colonists, however, were concerned that the baptism of slaves into their Puritan religion meant that the slaves would have to be freed. Puritans believed that no Christian could ever be considered a slave. By 1667, the Virginia colonial legislature put the issue to rest, declaring that, "conferring the baptisme doth not alter the condition of the person as to his bondage or freedome."

The rituals that the slaves brought over did not completely disappear. Most slaves accepted Christianity, but with aspects of their own distinct cultures, and found that their old religions were quite adaptable to the one forced upon them. They may have lost their drums, but they still could use their hands and feet to beat out rhythms. They may have lost their old songs and stories, <u>but they still retained the call and response style of singing, and applied it to the hymns and songs that they were forced to learn.</u> As African-Americans began to preach to their own more and more, an individual expression of spirit rapture called "shouting." It involves rhythmic dancing that harks back to the spirit possessions that *would occur during rituals performed in their homelands."*[1]

Essentially, these African slaves were demon worshippers that were forcibly taken from their homes to live as slaves for white, Protestant masters. The Protestants forced them to convert to Christianity, but they still maintained elements of their heathenism, mainly their music and worship rituals. The white "Christian" Americans shunned this style of music as fleshly and ungodly. This situation created two styles of music in America: White Traditional and Black Rhythmic. Although there were many slaves that rejected this music, the vast majority clung to this style as part of their racial and cultural identity.

If we fast forward to the mid 1900's, America was still racially segregated in almost every aspect of life despite the abolition of slavery. White and Black Americans lived in different neighborhoods, drank from different water fountains, used different restrooms, worked different jobs, and they still listened to different styles of music!

White Americans listened to traditional, country and folk music, while Black Americans listened to what was then called rhythm and blues. R&B music was largely considered immoral and unacceptable according to white culture because of its heathen origin. Frank Sinatra was once quoted as saying that rock music was, "the most brutal, ugly, degenerate, vicious form of expression it has been my displeasure to hear." In the late 1940's, this was all changed by a man named Alan Freed.

"One of the most important popularizers of rock and roll during the '50s, Alan Freed was the first disc jockey and concert producer of rock and roll. Often credited with coining the term rock and roll in 1951, ostensibly to avoid the stigma attached to R&B and so called race music, Freed opened the door to white acceptance of black music, eschewing white cover versions in favor of the R&B originals." [2]

All Alan Freed did was simply change the name of this music from "R&B" to "Rock and Roll", and in doing so, he was able to attract white audiences to the concerts he produced. Satan used Alan Freed to bring this heathen form of music out of the small jazz clubs of the deep south into mainstream American culture.

A few years later, Alan Freed admitted that this is exactly what he did when he said, "Rock and Roll is really swing with a modern name. It began on the levees and plantations, took in folk songs, and features blues and rhythm."

Initially, the vast majority of Americans were vehemently opposed to Rock and Roll. This was caused by the still strong influence of Fundamental, Bible believing Christianity in America. But as one generation moved on, another rose up and this generation came to accept this immoral, taboo form of music as normal. As the late Vance Havner used to say, "We simply got used to the dark."

"Rock music was not viewed favorably by most traditional and <u>fundamentalist</u> Christians when it

became popular with young people from the 1950s, although early rock music was often influenced by country and gospel music. Religious people in many regions of the United States did not want their children exposed to music with unruly, impassioned vocals, loud guitar riffs and jarring, hypnotic rhythms. Rock and roll differed from the norm, and thus it was seen as a threat. Often the music was overtly sexual in nature...Individual Christians may have listened to or even performed rock music in many cases, but it was seen as anathema to conservative church establishments, particularly in the American South."⁵

By the late 1950's everyone was listening to Rock and Roll with one major exception: Christians! A basic study of Christian history will easily find that Christian people have always been different than the lost world in all areas, in all generations, including music.

In the 1920's, Christians stood with Billy Sunday for the Prohibition of Liquor. In the 1940's, Christians could be found filling up tents at the local evangelistic crusade. Christians have always been different than the world in conversation, dress, and music. This has always been the norm; if you were a Christian, it was expected that you were supposed to be a relatively holy person that did not indulge in the vices of the world. At this point in history, Rock and Roll was literally invading the United States, but there was a remnant that was resisting this wicked advancement: Fundamental Christianity. Sadly, this would not last for long. The watershed moment that changed American church culture was when a young singer from Tupelo, Mississippi became successful as a musician. This young man's name was Elvis Presley. In 1956 Elvis appeared on NBC and CBS singing songs like, "You Ain't Nothin' But A Hound Dog" and "Don't be Cruel." As his career progressed, there was another side of Elvis that was revealed to the public. People were surprised to discover that the most famous musician of all time was also a professing Christian! "The King" was once a young Assembly of God boy that grew up in church and still loved Gospel music.

For the first time in American history, there was a man in mainstream music that was both secular and sacred, both lost and found, both Rock and Gospel. He was a perfect blend of both. This had never happened before. Christians liked him because he sang Gospel music. Non-Christians liked him because he sang Rock and Roll. He danced like an immoral, vulgar man, but off stage it was not unusual to pass him in a hotel hallway hearing him singing Amazing Grace. One night he would be seen openly using drugs at parties and the next night he would stand up at another party and tell everyone what he had read in the Bible that morning.

Joe Moscheo was a singer with the Imperials and was a personal friend to Elvis. He recently wrote a book called "The Gospel Side of Elvis" in which he reveals that Elvis Presley was not just your typical Rock Star. Moscheo was invited to promote his book and do an interview with the 700 club.

Ross: In the early part of the book you said people have talked enough about the negative side, so I want to emphasize another side. That's what the title says, The Gospel Side of Elvis, and story after story after story, he'd come off stage...He would literally call you guys together to have Gospel sessions that went for hours, sometimes all night long.

Moscheo: That's what he wanted to do. *There were like two parts.* There was Elvis, the superstar, and he went out on stage with his jumpsuits, and he was 'Elvis.' And then when he came off stage, he was Elvis Presley...that was brought up in the church, and he wanted to sing Gospel music.

It is the opinion of the author that the entire CCM movement began when Elvis Presley created the mindset in the American people that you can be a Rock Star and a devoted follower of Christ at the same time. Just as Marijuana is considered a "gateway drug", the music career of Elvis Presley was a "gateway" to the apostate "Christianity" that we have today. Up to the time of Elvis Presley, there had never been anyone in American History who had the nerve to say that they were a rock star and a follower of Jesus Christ at the same time.

"Every performer who ever performed in rock and roll or even close to it is lying if they tell you that they weren't influenced in some way or another by Elvis Presley. He turned the world around." - Mac Davis

In the 1950's, while Elvis was performing on television, a young man was watching him from his San Francisco home. This young man was named Larry Norman, the father of Contemporary Christian Music. Time Magazine once called Norman "the most significant artist in his field." His life would be used greatly in the next stage of the development of CCM.

"Norman was born on April 8, 1947, in Corpus Christi, Texas. At the age of 3, he relocated to San Francisco, California...and in the mid 50's became fascinated with the music of Elvis Presley."[4]

As a child, Larry Norman's family attended a black Pentecostal church and a Southern Baptist Church. Norman, at a young age, became very dissatisfied with traditional Christianity and the church altogether. Taking the mindset created in him by Elvis Presley, he decided that he wanted to find a new way to reach out to people by using the thing he loved the most: Rock and Roll. Norman was somewhat of a local celebrity in the Southern California Rock and Roll culture. He was a member of a band named "People!" Norman and "People!" were a frequent opener for major bands like Jimi Hendrix and the Doors. Many of the members of People! became steeped in Scientology which caused Norman to leave the band in 1968. In 1969, Larry Norman released what is considered to be the very first Christian Rock and Roll album, "Upon This Rock." It was said that "Upon this Rock" was *the album that first recruited rock in the service of salvation."* Although on the surface Larry Norman seems like a decent Christian man, a study of the life of Larry Norman reveals many strange and alarming issues:

1. Norman Had a Disdain for Traditional Music

In Michael McFadden's book, The Jesus Revolution, Norman is quoted as saying "Kids just don't want to listen to God's empty songs anymore."

In other words, Larry Norman believed that songs like Amazing Grace, It Is Well with My Soul, How Firm a Foundation, How Great Thou Art, Holy Holy Holy, Be Thou My Vision, Blessed Assurance, When I Survey the Wondrous Cross, Jesus Paid it All, How Firm A Foundation, Come Thou Fount, When I See the Blood are nothing more than "God's empty songs."

Norman wrote a song entitled, "Why Should The Devil Have All The Good Music?" In this song, he wrote:

I ain't knocking the hymns,
Just give me a song that has a beat;
I ain't knockin' the hymns,
Just give me a song that moves my feet;
I don't like none of those funeral marches
I ain't dead yet!

"Let the word of Christ dwell in you richly in all wisdom; teaching and admonishing one another in psalms and hymns and spiritual songs, singing with grace in your hearts to the Lord." Colossians 3:16

Many have debated about the definition of "psalms and hymns and spiritual songs", but no matter how you define those terms you have to admit that if a man wants a song that "moves my feet" and says, "I don't like none of those funeral marches" then he is fleshly and most definitely NOT a spiritual man.

"This I say then, Walk in the Spirit, and ye shall not fulfil the lust of the flesh. For the flesh lusteth against the Spirit, and the Spirit against the flesh: and these are contrary the one to the other: so that ye cannot do the things that ye would." Galatians 5:16-17

2. Norman Held Strange Theological Teachings.

Larry Norman was asked about his first album and said, *"Upon This Rock was written to stand outside the Christian culture. I tried to create songs for which there was no anticipated acceptance. I wanted to display the flexibility of the gospel and **that there was no limitation to how God could be presented**. I used abrasive humor and sarcasm as much as possible, which was also not a traditional aspect of Christian music. I chose negative imagery to attempt to deliver a positive message, like "I Don't Believe in Miracles" is actually about faith. "I Wish We'd All Been Ready" talked about something I had never heard preached from a pulpit as I grew up.*
*"The Last Supper" and "Ha Ha World" used very surreal imagery which drug users could assimilate. My songs weren't written for Christians. No, it was not a Christian album for those believers who wanted everything spelled out. It was more like a street fight. I was saying to Christians, **"I'm going to present the gospel, and I'm not going to say it like you want. This album is not for you."*** [6]

It is the opinion of the author that Larry Norman was a saved man, but woefully misguided in his approach to ministry. Norman seemed to be a man that was living in rebellion against what he was taught growing up in a Southern Baptist home. No doubt he developed this rebellious heart in the late 60's when his band "People!" was opening for Van Morrison, The Doors, The Who, Janis Joplin, and Jimi Hendrix. His rebellion was apparent in his music, long hair, and loose lifestyle, but it also showed itself in his theology.

When a man says he believes in the "flexibility of the gospel," then he is saying that he does not believe in the authority of the Bible or the parameters that the Bible places on the gospel. Any disregard for the authority of the Bible is rebellion. The danger in trying to "flex" the gospel is that man can very quickly find themselves preaching "another gospel."

*"I marvel that ye are so soon removed from him that called you into the grace of Christ unto **another gospel**: Which is not another; but there be some that trouble you, **and would pervert the gospel of Christ**. But though we, or an angel from heaven, preach any other gospel unto you than that which we have preached unto you, let him be accursed. As we said before, so say I now again, If any man preach any other gospel unto you than that ye have received, let him be accursed." -* Galatians 1:6-9

Norman also stated, that there was no limitation to how God could be presented. The theological error of this statement is so apparent that even someone with an elementary school level of Bible knowledge

21

could see what is wrong with it. The presentation of God in the Bible is very specific; the Bible teaches that the chief attribute of the Lord is His holiness.

When Moses met God in Exodus 3:5, the Lord told him that he was standing on *"holy ground."* When Joshua met the Lord in Joshua 5:15, he was commanded, *"Loose thy shoe from off thy foot; for the place whereon thou standest is holy."* When Hannah prayed to the Lord in 1 Samuel 2:2, she said, *"There is none holy as the Lord: for there is none beside thee."* When Isaiah saw the Lord in Isaiah 6:3, the Cherubim cried, *"Holy, holy, holy, is the Lord of hosts: the whole earth is full of his glory."*

When Jesus was met by a man with an unclean spirit in Mark 1:24, the demons said to Jesus, *"Let us alone; what have we to do with thee, thou Jesus of Nazareth? art thou come to destroy us? I know thee who thou art, the Holy One of God."* When Peter was addressing a crowd in Act 3:14, he declared about Jesus, *"But ye denied the Holy One and the Just, and desired a murderer to be granted unto you."*

Many times in the New Testament, the Spirit of God is called the "Holy Ghost" or the "Holy Spirit." The Bible never refers to God the Father, God the Son, or God the Spirit as "cool," "hip," "rad," "far out," "neat," "relevant," "right on," "swell," "savvy," "with it," "super," or "hunky dory." When discussing theology, we must use theological terms.

It is vital to present the Lord the way that the Bible

presents the Lord. God is Holy and to present a Holy God by using unholy means is impossible. To use unholy means to show a Holy God is to show an unholy god. Showing a Holy God with unholy means is likened to presenting a picture of Hillary Clinton on the gun range shooting an AK-47. Many would doubt the authenticity of that picture.

When statements like "there was no limitation to how God could be presented" are accepted by mainline "Christianity" then it soon becomes possible for God to be made into whatever image you can imagine No matter how unscriptural or heretical.

When men see who God is according to the Bible, they have to make a choice: either believe what the Bible teaches or make another "god" in their own mind.

"Professing themselves to be wise, they became fools, And changed the glory of the uncorruptible God into an image made like unto corruptible man..." Romans 1:22-23a

Norman was quoted in a 2004 documentary, "Why Should the Devil Have All the Good Music", as saying: "And if you end up writing artistic songs that don't mention Christ, if that's what God has inspired you to do, that's probably going to help people through the power of the Holy Spirit." [7]

Norman is saying that the Holy Spirit will help people through songs that don't mention Christ. This statement is one of the defining characteristics of the Christian rock world. Most Christian rock songs are simply love songs peppered with generic Christian clichés. ("Lord knows," "Give me Grace," "You are Everything," "All I Need is You"). Maybe this was the logic that Michael W. Smith used when he released the 1992 album "Change Your World." On this album, you will find only two songs that mention God and those references are so generic and vague that you would be intellectually dishonest to call this a "Christian" album.

3. Norman Had A Disdain For The Local Church.

If you met a man that claimed to be a doctor that had no use for clinics, hospitals, or modern medicine would you question his medical credentials? If you met a man claiming to be a pro-baseball player, but had rarely thrown a baseball, could not swing a bat, or hated going to a baseball game, would you question his legitimacy? If you met a person claiming to be a professional opera singer, but hated music and theaters, would you question their honesty? If you met a "Christian" musician that claimed he had no use for the Church, would you question their spirituality?

These are the questions that must be asked about Larry Norman when he makes the following statements: "I love God and I follow Jesus, but I just don't have much affinity for the organized folderol of the churches in the western world."[8]

"I didn't care about the church; I thought the church is already saved. What do I care what they think of me or if they ever hear any of my songs? This music is for non-believers." [7]

A brief study will show that there has never been anyone in the Bible or church history that was a serious Christian that did not regularly attend and love the Church.

"Not forsaking the assembling of ourselves together, as the manner of some is; but exhorting one another: and so much the more, as ye see the day approaching." Hebrews 10:25

"And they continued steadfastly in the apostle's doctrine and fellowship, and in breaking of bread, and in prayers." Acts 2:42

"So when they were dismissed, they came to Antioch: and when they had gathered the multitude together, they delivered the epistle: Which when they had read, they rejoiced for the consolation." Acts 15:30-31

"And upon the first day of the week, when the disciples came together to break bread, Paul preached unto them, ready to depart on the morrow; and continued his speech until midnight. And there were many lights in the upper chamber, where they were gathered together." Acts 20:7-8

"In the name of our Lord Jesus Christ, when ye are gathered together." 1 Corinthians 5:4

"And when he had considered the thing, he came to the house of Mary the mother of John, whose surname was Mark; where many were gathered together praying." Acts 12:12

"To gather with God's people in united adoration of the Father is as necessary to the Christian life as prayer." - Martin Luther

"The highest expression of the will of God in this age is the Church which He purchased with His own blood. To be scripturally valid, any religious activity must be part of the church. Let it be clearly stated that there can be no service acceptable to God in this age, that does not center in and spring out of the church. Bible schools, tract societies, Christian business men's committees, seminaries and the many independent groups working at one or another phase of religion, need to check themselves reverently and courageously, for they have no true spiritual significance outside of or apart from the church." - AW Tozer

"I know there are some who say, 'Well, I've given myself to the Lord, but I don't intend to give myself to any church.' I say, 'Now why not?' And they answer, 'Because I can be just as good a Christian without it.' I say, 'Are you quite clear about that? You can be as good a Christian by disobedience to your Lord's commands as by being obedient? There's a brick. What is the brick made for? It's made to build a house. It is of no use for the brick to tell you that it's just as good a brick while it's kicking about on the ground by itself, as it would be as part of a house. Actually, it's a good-for-nothing brick. So, you are rolling stone Christians; I don't believe that you're answering the purpose for which Christ saved you. You're living contrary to the life which Christ would have you live and you are much to blame for the injury you do." - Spurgeon

Does anyone see the irony in Spurgeon calling people "Rolling Stone" Christians?

Why would Larry Norman call himself a follower of Christ but admit that, "I didn't care about the church"? If God has given Norman a special "pass" to love Christ, but not love the Church, then it would be the first time in the history of Christianity that the Lord has done so.

"I was out to create a dialogue with people who believed they hated God. I wanted to be on the battlefield, fighting a spiritual battle, trying to convince and convert the undecided and get them to cross the battle line to stand together with other new believers. Though I may have been in error in standing aside from the brethren by not performing for them, the established Church was simply immaterial to me." [9]

4. Norman's Life Was Plagued with Accusations of Immorality.

In 2008, David Di Sabatino made the film "Fallen Angel: The Outlaw Larry Norman." In this documentary, Norman is portrayed as a vicious and ruthless businessman, a loose living, promiscuous wife stealer, and the claim is made that he fathered a child while on tour in Australia. Many of these claims have been disputed, and at this point, it is impossible to prove any immorality on his part. The only thing left to do is simply let the lewd artwork on the cover of Norman's albums speak for themselves.

Many would find it significant that, in 2001, two men were inducted into the Gospel Music Hall of Fame: Elvis Presley and Larry Norman.

The next major player in the history of Christian Rock was **Stryper**. They started out in an Orange County, California garage and were the first Christian Rock band to be played on MTV.

"Stryper's third album, 'To Hell With The Devil,' was released on October 24, 1986, and went platinum after spending three months on Billboard's album charts, eventually selling more than 2 million copies. In addition to being Stryper's most successful record, it was both the first contemporary Christian music and Christian Metal album to achieve this feat." [10]

A study of this band will show many strange similar issues to that of Larry Norman. First of all, they had serious morality issues. Michael Sweet, the leader of Stryper, did an interview with Jeb Wright in which he said: *"The key to it for us, concerning all things for us, is to just be real. When we go out to dinner with someone who is not a Christian and I order a beer or a glass of wine then you hear them gasp and they say,* "WHAT? YOU'RE CHRISTIAN?" I am, but I love beer and I love wine. I love a good cigar every now and then. I am free, man. That is not what being a Christian is about." [11]

Secondly, Stryper was often at odds with the Church. Michael Sweet said in an interview with The Quietus: "We didn't really turn our back on

28

Christianity, we just rebelled a bit towards the church because we'd gotten a lot of flak from them. It was a period in our lives when we decided, "You know what? We're not going to take this anymore." There were a handful of people that had really been speaking out against us year after year. So, we said, "Let's do our own thing, here's what we think about you" and we wrote the song 'Against The Law'. But we did it with a bit of a rebellious attitude which was wrong." [12]

Tim Gaines, the bassist of Stryper, eventually left the band because of the apparent inner struggle he had to justify what they were doing. "Were we there to take the praise and glory away from what God was doing? Were we really leading people to the saving knowledge of Jesus Christ or were we just putting on a show and receiving the glory for ourselves?" [13]

The lead guitarist of Stryper was named Richard Alfonso Martinez. Martinez prefered to go by his stage name "Oz Fox," in honor of his hero Ozzy Osbourne, the godfather of Heavy Metal. One of the most notable events in his life is when he married his second wife Annie Lobert. Lobert was a former prostitute for 16 years and now leads a ministry in Las Vegas, Nevada called "Hookers for Jesus." Yes, you read that correctly.

I would like to add here that I have several sources that cite that during the late 80s the lead singer of Stryper admitted that he was drunk for much of the "Against the Law" tour. Due to the fact that I am

29

unable to find an actual copy of this interview, I will not quote it in this edition of *Calling Evil Good.*

With the careers of Larry Norman and Stryper going full steam ahead, the Devil needed to attack the barrier between secular and sacred from another direction. He had already breached the gate with Rock and Roll, now it was time to finish the job with Pop music. It was at this time that Amy Grant came on the scene.

This young Church of Christ teenager was given her first recording contract five weeks before she turned 16. *Amy Grant*, the title of her first album, was released before she graduated high school. After achieving a great measure of success as a Christian musician, she fell to the purpose of Satan and became what she called a "crossover artist."

"In the mid-1980s, she began broadening her audience and soon became one of the first CCM artists to cross over into mainstream Pop, on the heels successful albums Unguarded and Lead Me On." [14]

"Amy Grant has bridged the gap between Christian and mainstream Pop." - CCM Magazine

Elvis Presley, Larry Norman, and Stryper's careers were all marred by immorality. Amy Grant was no different.

On January 18,1991, Grant released the most

popular song of her career: "Baby, Baby". Three months later, the music video of this hit single aired on MTV. The video shows this "Christian artist" flirting provocatively with a male actor in such a way that would make any red-blooded, self-respecting husband very upset.

"With Her song 'Baby Baby' (Amy Grant) is No. 1 this week on the billboard chart. The song was written about her 16-month-old daughter, Millie, but in the video, 'baby' is a flirty, touchy guy... Though she has bridged the chasm between Christian and pop genres, she insists she hasn't changed. The Baby Baby does give the song a sexier slant, but numerous references to Grant's religious faith remain." USA Today, April 22, 1991[15]

"Christians can be sexy. What I'm doing is a good thing." Grant, People Magazine, July 15, 1991[16]

"Tune in to any of the Christian cable programs and you won't have to wait long before some band, dressed in its best sequins and tuxedos, looking for all the world as if its last gig was at Caesar's Palace, will praise the Almighty in the same way Las Vegas praises the almighty dollar. They all make the same fatal mistake: that somehow the lyrics change the music's context, its subliminal message. More likely, the very opposite begins to happen: the Vegas/Wayne Newton lounge-act style is sanctified through its Christian associations (reverse effect). They sing about you– as in, "You Light Up My Life." All the listener has to do is fill in the blank: 'You' can be God, but it can also be a lover, a husband or a wife, a father or a mother, a dog or a cat. Lyrics aside, Grant uses all of the commercial weapons available, including sex, to promote her music. Maybe her come-hither look on the album cover really suggests that she wants to have you over to talk about God, but who is to know?" James Chute, professional music critic for the Milwaukee Journal

By the mid 90's the Pandora's box had been opened and only the Lord truly knows the spiritual damage that had been done to America. Satan was having a field day of misleading the masses by using his ultimate deception: The Merger of the Church and the World.

After all, why should the devil have all the good music?

Where Are We Now?

Since the 1950's, America has gone through many major changes. We changed politically, economically, socially, and most of all morally and spiritually. It is easy to see that America has slowly changed from a Christian nation to a secular nation. The 10 Commandments are being taken out of the courthouse, the Bible is no longer being taught in schools, football coaches are losing their jobs for praying with their local high school teams, etc.

During my research for this book, I found that even the secular world is noticing the sharp decline in American Christianity. Tobin Grant is a political science professor at Southern Illinois University and the Associate Editor of the Journal for the Scientific Study of Religion. He recently wrote an article called "The Great Decline: 60 Years of Religion in One Graph." His findings were astounding:

"The graph of this index tells the story of the rise and fall of religious activity. During the post-war, baby-booming 1950s, there was a revival of religion. Indeed, some at the time considered it a third great awakening. Then came the societal changes of the 1960s, which included a questioning of religious institutions. The resulting decline in religion stopped by the end of the 1970s, when religiosity remained steady. Over the past fifteen years, however, religion has once again declined. But this decline is much sharper than the decline of 1960s and 1970s. Church attendance and prayer is less frequent. The

number of people with no religion is growing. Fewer people say that religion is an important part of their lives. All measures point to the same drop in religion: If the 1950s were another Great Awakening, this is the Great Decline."[18]

Mark Chaves, a Harvard graduate, and Sociology Professor at Duke University published a paper called, "The Decline of American Religion?" In this paper, he points out several alarming studies about American Christianity.

"In Muncie, Indiana, the percentage of high school students who agreed with the statement, 'Christianity is the one true religion and everyone should be converted to it,' dropped from 91 percent in 1924 to 41 percent in 1977. Today, three quarters of Americans say "yes" when asked if they believe there is any religion other than one's own that offers a true path to God; 70 percent say that religions other than their own can lead to eternal life. Not only is the United States more religiously diverse than it was several decades ago; Americans also appreciate religious diversity more than they once did."

We also see a steep decline in the numbers of college students going into any type of ministry.

"Relatedly, a career in religious leadership is less attractive than it used to be, especially among young people. About 1 percent (10 in 1,000) of college freshmen expected to become clergy in the 1960s, declining to 0.3 percent (3 in 1,000) in the late 1980s, and remaining at about that level since then. That

means that the level of interest in a religious career among today's college freshmen is less than half what it was in 1970. This decline continues a very long-term trend. At the time of the Civil War, about 1 in 5 college graduates became clergy, declining to 6 percent by 1900."

Chaves even points out that there is an increase of people in America that simply don't believe in God at all.

"There is one more trend I want to mention. I have saved this trend for last because it is the one that is most likely to surprise even people who track trends in America. It also is the trend that leads most directly to the reflections I want to offer about future research on religious trends. I refer to the fact that there is a small, but unmistakable decline even in belief in God. Averaging GSS data between 1988 and 2008, 93 percent of people say they believe in God or a higher power. This percentage remains essentially constant, and very high over the 20 years it has been measured in the GSS. This very high and remarkably stable level of belief in God is well known. But a longer view shows something different. Tom W. Smith has combined various surveys to show that in the 1950s, 99 percent of Americans said they believed in God, and that number has dropped, slowly but steadily, to stand at 92 percent in 2008. This is a small decline that has stretched out over five decades, and after five decades of change nearly everyone still says they believe in God or a higher power. Still, change has occurred. It has occurred so slowly that it is difficult to see over even a two-decade span, but combining multiple surveys

over a longer period of time shows real decline. The percentage of Americans who say they are certain that God exists similarly looks stable over the 20 years it has been measured in the GSS, but shows decline if we combine multiple surveys conducted over a longer period of time. There are other trends in American religion, but none that contradict my basic conclusion that no indicator of traditional religious belief or practice is going up. There is more diffuse spirituality, but this diffuse spirituality should not be mistaken for an increase in traditional religiosity. On the contrary, every indicator of traditional religiosity is either stable or declining. Therefore, I think it is reasonable to conclude that American religion has in fact declined in recent decades – slowly, but unmistakably."[19]

This decline in American spirituality is caused by the lack of influence of the church (1 Peter 4:17). The church has become a place of convenience rather than conviction. Christians are supposed to be the salt of the earth, but many have become savorless (Matthew 5:11). One of the ways that the church has become savorless is in its music. The church now has brought the music of the heathen in, and therefore has become a third-rate imitation of the world. When the lost look and see the church acting like, living like, and singing like them, then they see no need to come to Christ. Their thinking becomes something like, "if they are just like me and are going to Heaven, then I must be going to Heaven too." If you think that is ridiculous, then I would like to inform you that I personally thought this for many years when I was a teenager. These worldly, rock and roll "Christians" were a great stumbling block in my salvation. I believe I would have been saved much sooner if it had not been for these people.

There was a time in America when you had two kinds of people in town: Sinners and Saints. The Christian Rock industry has been used by Satan to blur the line between these two types of people. This industry has basically created a perceived third kind of person that we will call the "Sinner Saint." These "Sinner Saints" claim to love the vices of the world and the Savior too. Their life is no different than the average unsaved American. The only difference is that they claim to believe in Christ, often to the surprise of their friends. These "Sinner Saints" have dwindled down New Testament salvation from a life changing, born again experience that causes you to live a life of relative holiness to simply an intellectual consent to the question: "Do you believe in God?" (James   2:19)

These people claim to be Christians and even pepper their language with supposed Christian clichés: "Thank God," "Grace of God," "Amen," "God Bless," And then live lives on par with the average lost person.

For the next few pages let's shine the light on some of the most famous American "Sinner Saints."

Beyonce Knowles

Basic Bio: Beyoncé Giselle Knowles-Carter is a native of Houston, TX. She began her career with a trio of women named "Destiny's Child," and then began a solo career in 2003. As of 2016, Beyonce has won 20 Grammy Awards for her music. She is married to famous rap star JayZ.

Sinner/Saint Qualifications: Despite her Methodist upbringing, Beyonce has lived a life of complete wickedness. Destiny's Child's first hit single was a song called, "No, No, No". A portion of the lyrics are:

Tell me what's goin' on
Tell me how you feel
'Cause boy I know you want me
Just as much as I want you
So come and get my love It's all here for you

Unfortunately, this lustful, lewd, and immoral trend would continue in the life and music of Beyonce. Destiny's Child's second album, "The Writing's on the Wall", would be filled with songs about fornication, adultery, and anger over adultery. Then they shamelessly added a track of the trio singing "Amazing Grace." Beyonce uses R-rated language in one track and then praises God in the next.

The next hit album by Destiny's Child was titled "Survivor." Track titles include Nasty Girl, Sexy Daddy, and then they included a track at the end of the album called "Gospel Medley."

There is much more that I could write about. Maybe I could tell you about her marriage to Jay Z, the filthy rap star that openly mocks the Bible, has people chant his name in worship during concerts, claims to have never read the Bible, and unbeknownst to many of his fans, his full stage name is Jay-Z-hova, a mockery of "Jehovah" (Psalm 83:18). Or maybe I could tell you that Beyonce has admitted to being possessed by a demon named "Sasha Fierce."

While Beyonce claims to be a Christian, her life tells a different story. She is a classic "Sinner Saint."

I hesitate to add this last story, but I think it needs to be included. Let me preface this by saying that I am a King James Bible only preacher. Someone once asked how the group Destiny's Child named themselves. Here is the story:

"We got that name out of the Bible. One day Beyonce's mom was about to read the Bible and she opened it up to read a scripture in Isaiah. Our picture fell out. Under our picture in bold-faced print was the word "destiny." At the time, we were looking for a name, so felt that God was sending us this name. We found out that a lot groups had the name, so we had "Child," as a rebirth of Destiny." [20]

The word "Destiny" does not appear in the King James Bible, but it does show up in the ASV, ESV, and the NIV. Being that the NIV is the most popular of these versions, I looked up this verse online. I was astounded to find that it said:

"But as for you who forsake the LORD and forget my holy mountain, who spread a table for Fortune and fill bowls of mixed wine for Destiny, I will destine you for the sword, and all of you will fall in the slaughter; for I called but you did not answer, I spoke but you did not listen. You did evil in my sight and chose what displeases me." - Isaiah 65:11-12 NIV

I will reiterate here that I am a King James Bible only preacher, but that is an eerie coincidence.

Alice Cooper

Basic Bio: Vincent Damon Furnier (aka Alice Cooper), a native of Arizona, is considered by many to be "The Godfather of Shock Rock." Many of his shows featured electric chairs, fake blood, and chopping heads off baby dolls. Gary Blackman said about his band that they "first introduced horror imagery to rock and roll, and whose stagecraft and showmanship have permanently transformed the genre." Furnier's band was inducted into the Rock and Roll Hall of Fame in 2011.

Sinner/Saint Qualifications: Furnier was originally the lead singer of the band "Alice Cooper," but when he went solo he purchased the rights of the band's name and is now referred to as "Alice Cooper". Furnier was raised in a fundamental Mormon home where his father was the local minister. Furnier's life was one of vice and drug addiction. Furnier claims that his wife, Sheryl Goddard, left him over his alcoholism in 1980, but they reconciled after he quit drinking in 1981.

Furnier claims to have become a born again Christian in 1980, but many problems arise when you research his testimony. First of all, his testimony is erroneous and vague:

"God's chipping away at your life all the time to try to make you more like Him," said Cooper. "That's what a Christian is, a person that's being molded and shaped all their life .... I think the Lord expects you to do your best in His name." [21]

Despite quitting drugs and drinking, his life is basically the same as it was in his early career. Furnier has cleaned up his music some, but he still uses the extremely macabre imagery in his performances. As I was reading a website about his supposed conversion and faith, I found a paragraph that sums up the "Sinner Saint" life of Furnier brilliantly:

"In an interview with the evangelical Christian program The Harvest Show, Alice Cooper said that if there is a Bible story that represents his life, it is Jonah and the whale. He also disclosed that despite the dark and demonic aspects of some of his early music, there were still Christian messages being conveyed about good vs. evil and that the songs did warn against Satan." [22]

In other words, Furnier tries to say that his songs did contain a warning against Satan, despite the fact that he was chopping the heads off of baby dolls while he was singing. Essentially, he is "Calling Evil Good."

R. Kelly

Basic Bio: Robert Sylvester Kelly, a native of Chicago, IL is a famous R&B artist and is most well-known for his song "I Believe I Can Fly," for which he won three Grammys. In March 2011, Billboard named R. Kelly "the most successful R&B artist of the last 25 years." Kelly has also been given nicknames like "King of R&B" and "King of Soul."

Sinner/Saint Qualifications: Kelly's life is probably the most immoral of all those mentioned in this chapter. Kelly has been charged with 14 counts of child pornography in Illinois, was going to be charged in Florida, but a judge ruled that the evidence was obtained illegally, and many of his former assistants have come forward and said that he has raped at least 24 teenage girls.

"Jim DeRogatis, the Chicago Sun-Times reporter who covered the allegations against R. Kelly more thoroughly than anyone else, said in 2013 that he had interviewed close to two dozen women who claimed the famed R&B singer sexually abused them. Virtually all of the allegations are said to have occurred in or near Chicago, where Kelly is from, and involve claims Kelly repeatedly pursued minors for sex. As the Daily Beast's, Goldie Taylor noted, Kelly's former friend and assistant Demetrius Smith observed in the memoir The Man Behind the Man: "Underage girls had proven to be his weakness He was obsessed, sickly addicted." [22]

In my research, I found an interesting article about the wicked lifestyle of Kelly. Lincoln Anthony Blades, an agnostic blogger, wrote an article entitled: Keep It REAL with Yourself: Are You R. Kelly Saved?! The premise of this article is that R Kelly says he is saved, but lives a very immoral life. He is not truly saved, but rather "R. Kelly Saved". In other words, he is what I refer to as a "Sinner Saint".

Many other accounts of his wicked lifestyle are his transgender daughter, his endorsement of Pro-Choice candidate Barack Obama, and a host of songs with titles that are incredibly lewd. It is also notable that in 2004, Kelly released an album called "Happy People/You Saved Me" in which he sings a song called "Surrender." Lyrics to this song include: "Give your life to God and all that, Y'know, that's good and I believe in God (I surrender to you Lord)."

In the same year, he released an album called "Unfinished Business" in which he sings a song called "She's Coming Home With Me." To call R Kelly a "Sinner Saint" is being extremely nice. The real tragedy is that there are multitudes of people that see nothing wrong with this man. For the sake of brevity, we will discontinue this list with R. Kelly.

The "Sinner Saint" culture of America used to be isolated to a few extreme examples, but now it has become so popular to be a "Sinner Saint" that almost every celebrity in every area of the entertainment industry claims to be a Christian. Celebrities that are in this category are: Lil Wayne, Faith Hill, Tyler Perry, Carrie Underwood, Whitney Houston, Gary Busey, Denzel Washington, Toby Keith, Lenny Kravitz, Brad Paisley, Alan Jackson, Vince Gil, James Brown, Joseph Simmons, U2, Black

Sabbath, Evanescence, Kings of Leon, POD, Katy Perry, and Hulk Hogan. I want you to read the next paragraph VERY CAREFULLY! This paragraph sums up the whole of this book. If you miss the truth of this paragraph, then you will miss the entire point of this book.

The Satanic deception is simply this: <u>blur the line between the lost and the saved so that the lost think that they are saved.</u> This satanic deception is going to be responsible for the damnation of millions of Americans at the great white throne judgement. Sadly, we will find out that the "Sinner Saint" is not half lost and half saved, but he is rather ALL lost and too blinded by his own religiosity to know it.

I believe the reason that America is in such bad shape morally is because the church is in such bad shape spiritually. The reason the church is in such bad shape spiritually is because the church has become worldly. The reason the church has become worldly can be attributed to many things, but one of the main reasons can be found in their use of the world's music.

When I was a kid growing up in Atlanta, I remember the different genres of music that my friends and family listened to. There was Country, Rock, Rap, and Christian music. There was ALWAYS a difference between them. This is no longer the case today. Today we have people that are "crossover" musicians. We have Christian Country, Christian Rock, and Christian Rap.

This is because the line between secular and sacred has been destroyed. When a man tries to merge the secular and the sacred, Then he proves that to him nothing is truly sacred.

This "merger" mentality has bled over into nearly all areas of the Christian world. We have a generation that takes anything, no matter how immoral, and places the word "Christian" in front of it and declares it sacred. We have Christian Beer, Christian Night Clubs, Christian Pro Athletes, Christian Rock, Christian Rap, and Christian Country.

We have lost the division. We cannot tell where the church begins and the world ends. The goal of the great commission was to bring a holy bride of Christ out of the world, but now we have so much of the world in the church that being a Christian has become almost meaningless.

At some point, somebody has to draw a line and say that "this is Christianity" and "this is not." These "Sinner Saints" are taking anything imaginable (swimming, horseback riding, rock music, rap music, diets, workout routines, charities, and dance routines) and adding the word "Christian" to it and saying that it is acceptable in the eyes of the Lord.

For example, there is a woman in Texas that holds "Christian Pole Dancing" classes in her studio. These women meet in a building with poles set up and do provocative pole dancing to "Christian Music." Where will we draw the line? Is there no line anymore?

The most popular show on cable TV in 2014 was Duck Dynasty. The Robertson family are members of the Church of Christ denomination. The theological term for a Church of Christ member is a Cambellite. Cambelites believe that baptism by immersion is essential for salvation. The Roberson family has adopted the "Sinner Saint" lifestyle and can be seen gambling, and making alcoholic drinks on their show. The Robertson family has even come out with their own brand of "Christian" alcohol. Duck Dynasty wine. Does drinking this make you a Christian drunk?

The insanity of this entire movement became real to me when I was watching the news in the spring of 2014. There was a news program in Louisville, Kentucky that was covering an upcoming event called "Walk on Water." This was a "Christian" rock concert that is played on the banks of the Ohio River every year. The host of the news program introduced the band and then asked what song they would be playing. Their response was: "We will be playing 'Don't Stop Believing' by Journey." I sat before my TV in disbelief as I watched a "Christian" band play a secular rock song on TV and claim that it was Christian music. Here are the words to this song:

Just a small town girl
Livin' in a lonely world
She took the midnight train goin' anywhere
Just a city boy
Born and raised in south Detroit
He took the midnight train goin' anywhere
A singer in a smoky room
A smell of wine and cheap perfume
For a smile they can share the night
It goes on and on, and on, and on

Strangers waiting
Up and down the boulevard
Their shadows searching in the night
Streetlights, people
Livin' just to find emotion
Hidin' somewhere in the night
Working hard to get my fill
Everybody wants a thrill
Payin' anything to roll the dice
Just one more time
Some will win, some will lose
Some were born to sing the blues
Oh, the movie never ends
It goes on and on, and on, and on.

If you will notice a few things: Christ is not mentioned. No clear Bible references are mentioned; no Christian themes are mentioned. If a vague reference to something remotely spiritual determines that a song is Christian, then Slayer would have to be the most Christian band of all time.

Slayer album titles include: "Hell Awaits," "South of Heaven," "Divine Intervention," and "Repentless."

"Her priests have violated my law, and have profaned mine holy things: they have put no difference between the holy and profane, neither have they shewed difference between the unclean and the clean, and have hid their eyes from my sabbaths, and I am profaned among them." Ezekiel 22:26

I think that it is appropriate here to note that Larry Norman said about his album, "Upon this Rock," in 1972 that, "It was too religious for the rock and roll stores and too rock and roll for the religious stores."

WHY DOES THIS MATTER?

So far we have learned how Contemporary Christian Music came into existence and the end fruit of Contemporary Christian Music produces a culture of Sinner Saints. Now, let's talk about why this is important.

The issue of music matters because the character of God matters. The church is supposed to be a representation of the character of God on earth (1 Peter 2:9-10, 2 Corinthians 5:20, Ephesians 2:10). If we misrepresent who the Lord is, then we commit treason against Heaven and undermine our chances to win the lost with the gospel.

When God's people fail to live holy lives, then they project that the God of Christianity is not holy. A true understanding of the Holiness of God is essential for mankind to be saved. Man does not know that he needs a Savior until he realizes how unholy he is in the light of the Holiness of God (Isaiah 6). He cannot be saved until he sees himself as unclean and separate from God (Romans 1:29-32, Romans 3:10-19, Romans 5:12, Romans 6:23).

As a teenager, I was around many religious people, but my family never went to church. I remember one school year that I was the only one in my class that did not regularly attend church. I remember hearing things about God on many occasions. I remember hearing my classmates sing about God on a few occasions. I even remember seeing some of my classmates bring their Bibles to school, but I also remember their lifestyles. There was no difference in their lives from mine. They said the same cuss words, had the same worldly vices, listened to the same music, and dressed the same way that I did. (Keep in mind that I was not saved at this time).

One occasion specifically sticks out in my mind. I remember being in ninth grade at Dacula High School. Our biology teacher decided to have Biology class in the park across the street from the school that day. So, we went to the park and talked about plants for the duration of the class period. I remember a small group of girls were singing "Our God Is An Awesome God" in harmony. These kids were raised in a very large evangelical Southern Baptist Church in our town. The sad part of this story is that I knew that ALL of those girls drank alcohol at parties.

These people did unspeakable damage to my soul without even realizing it. I saw no need to come to their Savior because of their lifestyles. If these people that were just like me were going to Heaven, then I thought I was going too.

Jesus spoke to his disciples in Matthew 6 about prayer and the Christian life. "But if thine eye be evil, thy whole body shall be full of darkness. If therefore the light that is in thee be darkness, how great is that darkness!" Matthew 6:23

There is no lack of spiritual darkness in the world (Hinduism, Buddhism, Islam, Roman Catholicism, Scientology), but the darkest darkness there is, exists when those who claim the name of Christ walk in darkness. There are literally multitudes in Hell today who would have come to Christ had it not been for the wicked, worldly lifestyle of a "Christian" they knew personally. Anton Levey, the founder of the Church of Satan, claims that he left Christianity because of the worldly, inconsistent lifestyles of the Christians he personally knew.

I walked in utter spiritual confusion all my life. It was only until I was around some Godly, Separated, Spirit-filled, Christian people that I finally saw a need to be saved. By the time I was 17, I had never read the Bible, but I had read the lives of God's people (2 Corinthians 3:2). I later found out that the message of their lives was not the message of the Bible. This is why this book matters! If the Church continues to imitate the world in its lifestyle and music, then the Church will misrepresent God to the damnation of those around them.

The problem with American Christianity is that they are trying to be a "new creature" (2 Corinthians 5:17) while still loving their "old sins" (2 Peter 1:9). They claim they are a "new man" (Colossians 3:10), but have never put off the "old man" (Colossians 3:9). They claim to be "the unleavened bread of sincerity and truth" (1 Corinthians 5:8), but they are swollen with the old leaven of malice and wickedness (1 Corinthians 5:8). These people claim that their "old man is crucified with him" (Romans 6:6), but their lives and music are so similar to the world that any jury would have a hard time declaring them guilty of being a Christian.

This is the work of Satan. Blur the line between Right

and Wrong, Sin and Righteousness, Heaven and Hell, the World and the Church. Blend everything in together so that no difference can be seen in the eyes of the lost heathen. If you were to speak to the average 20-year-old on the campus of any major university they would tell you that there is no such thing as absolute truth! They believe this because many of them have NEVER known a Christian that lived an obedient, holy, and separated life unto God.

Satan laughs when a Church tries to put the new wine of Christianity into the old bottle of Rock and Roll. He then rejoices when the bottles perish and there is no longer the wine of testimony and witness for Christ in a sinner's life. Satan loves it when a Church takes the new cloth of Christianity and tries to sew it onto the old garment of Rock and Roll. He knows that the rent (tear) is made worse by doing so and that more people will be in Hell by a misrepresentation of Christianity than by no representation of Christianity (Matthew 9:16).

Years ago, I saw a flyer for a "Christian Rock" concert at a restaurant in my town. I called the youth pastor of the church and asked him if I could come and interview the bands on camera. I was given permission and even given VIP/backstage passes to the event. I walked into a gym called "The Cave" at this church and was immediately assaulted with loud, unskilled, heavily distorted, rock guitar music. There were hundreds of teens in this gym and they were all crowded up to a stage where groups of 14 to 21 year olds were playing rock music with their bands. A friend of mine accompanied me as we stayed for hours observing the behavior of the people. I found that the behavior, music, and spirit of the event were IDENTICAL to the behavior, music, and spirit of the many Rock concerts I had been to as a teenager before I was saved. I watched in horror as a group of 14-17-year-old boys walked off stage after playing the only three songs they knew to meet dozens of teenage girls screaming their names, asking for autographs, and emitting shrieks of ecstasy! The scene was IDENTICAL to the videos I had seen of young women screaming when the Beatles played live in concert and the videos of tweens screaming when they lay eyes upon Justin Beiber. I felt sick.

The band members told me that their favorite places to play were in bars, not in churches. They told me the names of the churches they were members of, but could not tell me what their church believed. They told me that their purpose in music was not to get people saved, but to make a positive connection with young people and plant seeds in their hearts. (Yes, they actually told me their goal was not to get people saved). They told me that their songs did not present the Gospel, but did have "biblical undertones."

One group told me that they had not been to church in months because they had been so busy playing gigs in bars and pool halls that they could not make a church service. One honest young musician told me that he is doing everything he can to imitate the mannerisms and musical style of Marilyn Manson. I applaud his honesty because he certainly is not trying to imitate Jesus Christ. I left the concert early and went to sit in my car. I was horrified at how woefully misguided these people were. Is this Christianity? Is this how the Lord intended the Church to be? How could these people know the Lord and be so wrong about this issue? How could these people call themselves Christians when there is little to no evidence that they are saved?

I went home that night and did the only thing I knew to do: read the Bible. I found several things that I will share with you in this chapter.

The first thing that the Lord showed me was that Satan is a master at imitating the things of God.

"How art thou fallen from heaven, O Lucifer, son of the morning! how art thou cut down to the ground, which didst weaken the nations! For thou hast said in thine heart, I will ascend into heaven, I will exalt my throne above the stars of God: I will sit also upon the mount of the congregation, in the sides of the north: I will ascend above the heights of the clouds; I will be like the most High." Isaiah 14:12-14

In my study of the Bible, I have found that Lucifer is not able to DESTROY truth, so he tries to DISTORT truth. Lucifer cannot PURGE the world of truth, so he PERVERTS the truth in the world. He cannot TEAR down truth so he tries to TAINT the truth. This is what I was seeing at that Christian Rock concert! Tainted, distorted, perverted, so called "Christianity!" That is why I was never saved at any of these events when I was a teenager! God was not the author of these events!

I struggled with this for a while. I kept asking the Lord, "How could these people not be of God when they are so nice?"

"And no marvel; for Satan himself is transformed into an angel of light. Therefore it is no great thing if his ministers also be transformed as the ministers of righteousness; whose end shall be according to their works." 2 Corinthians 11:14-15

Many of you reading this book are asking the question, "What does this have to do with Christian Rock?" The issue is that historically there has always been a division between the things of God and the things of the world. In the Bible, we see a division between God and Satan, the Flesh and the Spirit, Israel and the Philistines, Saved and Lost, Holy and Unholy, Belief and Unbelief, Heaven and Hell, Truth and Error, etc. The issue with Christian Rock is that it tries to be both: Holy and Unholy at the same time. Christian Rock tries to be Holy in an Unholy way.

Example: If I was at a church and I heard a missionary speak about having an evangelistic meeting that costs $5,000 and I wrote him a check for the cost, did I do well? YES! Let's say that I heard the missionary speak about having an evangelistic meeting that costs $5,000 and I did not have the money. I then left the church, robbed a bank at gunpoint for $5,000, came back to the church and gave him the $5,000. Did I do well? NO! You can try to help the cause of Christ in the wrong way and end up hurting the cause of Christ. This is in essence the logic of Christian Rock. I am going to reach people by doing things that are contrary to the clear teachings of the Bible. In other words: I am going to try to do the right thing with the wrong means. What more can I say? Do the ends justify the means?

Would it bother you that there is a Church in Fort Worth, Texas called "The Pub Church," where members meet in the Chimera Brewing Company on Sunday nights to play Christian Rock, drink beer, and preach the Bible? Would it bother you that the slogan of the "Pub Church" was "For The Wicked and Thirsty?" Would it bother you if I told you that the First Christian Church of Portland, Oregon has a ministry called "Beer & Hymns"?

The problem is not that these people don't mean well, but that they are trying to do the RIGHT thing the WRONG way! They are not obedient to the Word of God, but self-willed do-gooders void of the approval of Heaven. These self-righteous, religious false teachers are spending their lives DECEIVING and being DECEIVED. They serve the two-fold purpose of Satan: damning themselves and damning others. This is the issue. Most of these people are going to Hell, and they are taking multitudes with them (2 Timothy 3:13).

Read the following verses and consider the fact that God wants his church to be separate from the world:

"Be ye not unequally yoked together with unbelievers: for what fellowship hath righteousness with unrighteousness? and what communion hath light with darkness? And what concord hath Christ with Belial? or what part hath he that believeth with an infidel? And what agreement hath the temple of God with idols? for ye are the temple of the living God; as God hath said, I will dwell in them, and walk in them; and I will be their God, and they shall be my people. Wherefore come out from among them, and be ye separate, saith the Lord, and touch not the unclean thing; and I will receive you, And will be a Father unto you, and ye shall be my sons and daughters, saith the Lord Almighty." 2 Corinthians 6:14-18

In the above verses, we learn that we are not able to have fellowship with the Lord and have fellowship with the world at the same time. To be truly right with the Lord is to be wrong with the world. A married man cannot have the right relationship with his wife if he is flirting with another woman at the same time. The application that we can make here is that the church cannot be in the right relationship with Christ while flirting with Rock and Roll. You either love one or the other, not both.

"...and to keep himself unspotted from the world." James   1:27

"As obedient children, not fashioning yourselves according to the former lusts in your ignorance: But as he which hath called you is holy, so be ye holy in all manner of conversation; Because it is written, Be ye holy; for I am holy." - 1 Peter 1:14-16

"I wrote unto you in an epistle not to company with fornicators: Yet not altogether with the fornicators of this world, or with the covetous, or extortioners, or with idolaters; for then must ye needs go out of the world. But now I have written unto you not to keep company, if any man that is called a brother be a fornicator, or covetous, or an idolater, or a railer, or a drunkard, or an extortioner; with such an one no not to eat. For what have I to do to judge them also that are without? do not ye judge them that are within? But them that are without God judgeth. Therefore put away from among yourselves that wicked person." - 1 Corinthians 5:9-13

"And be not conformed to this world:but be ye transformed by the renewing of your mind, that ye may prove what is that good, and acceptable, and perfect, will of God." - Romans 12:2

When considering the topic of Rock and Roll used to praise the Lord, one must consider the question of Job in Job 14:4: "Who can bring a clean thing out of an unclean? not one."

IS MUSIC AMORAL?

The word "Amoral" is defined as: not involving questions of right or wrong; without moral quality; neither moral nor immoral. Essentially, amoral means that there is nothing inherently right or wrong with it. Examples of amoral acts are things like breathing, walking, lifting your arm, or balling up your fist. Objects that are amoral are things like money, the letters of the alphabet, notes on a piano, and knives. These things in themselves are not moral, but they can be used together to do immoral things.

There is nothing wrong with walking, breathing, and lifting your arm, while having a balled-up fist. The immorality comes when you walk into a store, lift your arm up to the clerk with a knife in your balled-up fist and use your breath to say "Give me all the Money!!!" There is nothing moral or immoral about the letters of the alphabet, but you can arrange the letters of the alphabet to make immoral words.

Much of American Evangelical Christianity has adopted the lie and logical fallacy that music is amoral. Frank Breeden, President of the Gospel Music Association, is one of the most vocal proponents of this lie and has even written about it.

"In his book Controversies of the Music Industry (2001), Richard D. Barnet states, "many fundamentalist religious groups and denominations decry rock music in general. Such groups may

consider established contemporary Christian artists such as Amy Grant, Petra, Steve Green and Twila Paris as reprehensible as secular bands like White Zombie and Marilyn Manson. And that, Christian rock bands too have come under criticism for supposedly promoting Satanism.Barnet asserts that Christian rock acts are controversial because they do not meet the Fundamental Evangelistic Association's (FEA) criteria for a truly "Christian" song.

That is, it must be doctrinally correct according to the FEA's interpretation of the Bible; it should not contain syncopation ("Does it stir the flesh to 'boogie,' or the spirit to praise the Lord?"), and it must be politically correct ("The character of much what is called "Christian" music may best be characterized as charismatic, universalist, socialist, utopian, idealistic."). Organizations such as Dial-the-Truth Ministries believe Christian rock bands fail to adhere to the prohibitions of II Corinthians 6:14, which instructs Christians against uniting the righteous with the unrighteous. Despite such criticism, Barnet concludes: "It should be noted that Christian rock also has millions of supporters, even among the ministry." Frank Breeden, President of the Gospel Music Association, the organization behind the Dove Awards, states that **"There really is no such thing as a Christian B-flat. Music in itself is an amoral vehicle."**[24]

The logical fallacy of this statement is easily observed. What Breeden is saying is that the note B-flat is not immoral so all music containing a B-flat is not immoral. This is the same as saying the letter "F" is not immoral, so therefore it is impossible to create a word starting with letter "F" that would be immoral. We all know that this is simply not so. The morality of a song is not created by an individual note, but rather by the compiling of notes in a sequence to create a song. The same is true about the letters of the alphabet. There is nothing immoral about the letter "D", but if you sequence many letters together with the letter "D" you can quickly create something that many consider immoral.

The principle is simply this: the single elements of music (notes, chords, rhythm) are not immoral in themselves, but they can be combined in such a way that is immoral. There are three major areas where music affects a person: behavior, mood, and morality:

Behavior

When I was a lost teenager I learned a great lesson about the behavioral effects of music. As I was riding in a car with a friend of mine, the radio began to play a new popular song by a rap artist. My friend turned up the music and asked me if I had heard this song before. As I listened to the song I noticed that my mood began to change. I began to feel angry and arrogant. It was then that I realized that I did not feel this way before the music began, but after! As the months went on, I noticed that people that constantly listened to this type of music behaved completely different in a social setting than those that did not. This principle is true of all types of music.

"Rock and roll music, if you like it, if you feel it, you

can't help but move to it. That's what happens to me. I can't help it." - Elvis Presley

Not only can music affect your social behavior it can also affect your financial behavior. A famous study by Ronald E. Milliman in 1982, published in the Journal of Marketing found that when background music was played in a supermarket, shoppers spent 34% more time there and spent more money. I know this to be true of my own life. I was working for Dillard's when I was in college, the music they played was soft pop. When I left that job, my wife noticed immediately that my spending habits changed drastically. I believe it is because I was no longer being influenced by that music.

Mood

Have you ever gotten into an elevator that was playing dark heavy metal music? No? Every elevator that you and I have ever been in has always played a soft, happy tune of music. This is because many people find being confined in a small space extremely uncomfortable and so the elevator companies had to find a way to put people at ease. The two major solutions they found were to put mirrors in the elevator, to make the elevator seem bigger, and to play soft music. Soft music has been scientifically proven to comfort people.

In the Old Testament, Saul had an evil spirit upon his life and he was looking for a man to come and play a song to help him spiritually. David, the future king of Israel, came and played a song on the harp and it changed the spirit and mood of King Saul. *"And it* came to pass, when the evil spirit from God was upon Saul, that David took an harp, and played with his hand: _so Saul was refreshed, and was well,_ and the evil spirit departed from him." 1 Samuel 16:23

In 2015, my home church was able to start a Christian radio station. Our station plays Christ honoring, uplifting music 24 hours a day. Not long after the radio station started, I was going around town running some errands that were very unpleasant to me. I was stressed about the pressures that I was under and it was bothering me. After listening to the Christ honoring music on the radio for a few hours I found myself in a much better spirit. I was helped by the kind of music I was listening to; in other words, the music changed my mood!

Morality

When people meet for the first time they often ask three basic questions: where one another is from, what do they do for a living, _and what kind of music they listen to_. The reason people do this is because the kind of music you listen to is often a direct reflection of the kind of person you are. In other words, music dictates your morals.

Not only is this my view, it is also the view of many great men of the past. Many philosophers and historians have claimed that the music of a nation can and will always dictate the morality of a nation. "Music can both establish and destroy morality. For no path is more open to the soul for the formation thereof than through the ears. Therefore, when the rhythms and moods have penetrated even to the soul through these organs, it cannot be doubted that they affect the soul with their own character and conform it to themselves." - Anicius Boethius, 6th Century Christian Philosopher

"Music can be intoxicating. Such apparently slight causes destroyed Greece and Rome, and will destroy England and America." - Henry David Thoreau"

Possibly the greatest weakness of the modern materialistic outlook upon the world is its inability to perceive the causes behind effects. If anywhere, it is here that the philosophers of ancient China, India, Egypt and Greece deserve our fullest respect, since it could be said that they specialized in seeing to the cause and core of things. And they most certainly would have agreed with Thoreau, that music can destroy civilization."[25] - David Tame

I believe that much of the social sins of American culture can be traced back to the type of music that is being listened to.

IS ROCK AND ROLL

MORAL MUSIC?

In chapter one we covered the history of Rock and Roll and we discovered that the origin of it being the pagan religions of the African slaves that came to America. We also covered that music can and does dictate your behavior, mood, and morals. In this chapter, let me give you two main reasons why Rock and Roll is a wicked, immoral kind of music.

1. The Lifestyle of the Artists Themselves

Let us go straight to the horse's mouth and see what kind of people that the American Rock and Roll industry is producing. Let us review some quotes from the leaders of the Rock and Roll community.

"Christianity will go. It will vanish and shrink. I needn't argue with that; I'm right and I will be proved right. We're more popular than Jesus now; I don't know which will go first, Rock and Roll or Christianity." - John Lennon

"Elvis may be the King of Rock and Roll, but I am the Queen." - Little Richard

"Rock and Roll keeps you in a constant state of juvenile delinquency." -Eddie Spaghetti

"Christians are a lot like dinosaurs – about to become extinct." - Marilyn Manson

"A kid once said to me 'Do you get hangovers?' I said, "To get hangovers you have to stop drinking." - Ian "Lemmy" Kilmister of Motorhead

"I wake up: I am mental, I got to bed and I am mental, I am mental within my dreams, I am mental within my normal state, I'm out of my mind." - Joey Jordison of Slipknot

"The only negative thing about murder is that when you kill someone they can no longer suffer" - Varg Vikernes of Mayhem

"I used to jog but the ice cubes kept falling out of my glass." - Dave Lee Roth of Van Halen

"I'm not God but if I were God, ¾ of you would be girls, and the rest would be pizza and beer." - Axl Rose of Guns n Roses

"I'm a family oriented guy; I've personally started four or five this year." - David Lee Roth of Van Halen

"Rock and Roll is about drugs." - Marilyn Manson

"We've all got our self-destructive bad habits, the trick is to find four or five you personally like the best and just do those all the time." - David Lee Roth of Van Halen

"It will be funny in about 10 years." - Ian "Lemmy" Kilmister of Motorhead on the events of September 11th, 2001

"Anyone who thinks they're happy should really see a doctor, because there is no reason to be happy." - Marilyn Manson

"I was living it. That's all there is to it. It was my life, that fusion of magic and music. Yes, I knew what I was doing. There's no point in saying about it, because the more you discuss it, the more eccentric you appear to be. But the fact is, as far as I was concerned, it was working, so I used it! I'll leave this subject by saying the four musical elements of Led Zeppelin making a fifth is magic into itself. That's the alchemical process." - Jimmy Page

"I really wish I knew why I've done some of the things I've done over the years. Sometimes I think that I'm possessed by some outside spirit. A few years ago, I was convinced of that, I thought I truly was possessed by the devil. I remember sitting through 'The Exorcist' a dozen times, saying to myself, 'Yeah, I can relate to that.'" - Ozzy Ozbourne

"Trying to seduce an audience is the basis of Rock and Roll, and if I may say so, I'm pretty good at it."
- Jon Bon Jovi

"All the songs we do are basically about one of three things: booze, sex, or Rock and Roll."
- Bon Scott, AC/DC

"I heard that your brain stops growing when you start doing drugs. Let's see, I guess that makes me 19." - Steven Tyler

"I'm just a musical prostitute, my dear." - Freddie Mercury

If that was not enough evidence for you, let me give you a short list of just **SOME** of the famous Rock and Roll stars who died because of their immoral lifestyle:

Rock Star	Cause of Death	Date of Death
Rudy Lewis	Drug Overdose	May 20, 1964
Dickie Pride	Drug Overdose	March 26, 1969
Jimi Hendrix	Asphyxiation caused by Drug Overdose	September 18, 1970
Janis Joplin	Heroin Overdose	October 4, 1970
Baby Huey	Drug Related Heart Attack	October 28, 1970
Jim Morrison	Drug Related Heart Failure (Disputed)	July 3, 1971
Gram Parsons	Morphine and Alcohol Overdose	September 19, 1973
Tim Buckley	Heroin Overdose	June 29, 1975

Keith Moon	Heroin Overdose	September 7, 1978
Sid Vicious	Heroin Overdose	February 2, 1979
Jimmy McCulloch	Morphine Poisoning	September 27, 1979
Bon Scott	Alcohol Poisoning	February 19, 1980
Lester Bangs	Darvon Overdose	April 30, 1982
Ricky Wilson	Complications with AIDS	October 12, 1985
Steve Clark	Overdose of Pain Killers	January 8, 1991
Freddie Mercury	Complications with AIDS	November 24, 1991
Ray Gillen	Complications with AIDS	December 1, 1993
Bradley Nowell	Heroin Overdose	May 25, 1996
Rob Pilatus	Alcohol and Pill Overdose	April 2, 1998
Kevin DuBrow	Cocaine Overdose	November 19, 2007
Amy Winehouse	Alcohol Poisoning	July 23, 2011

Please keep in mind that this is just a short list of those who have died because of their immorality. There are literally hundreds more that I chose not to put on this list.

2. The Themes and Lyrics of Rock and Roll Music

If the wicked, immoral lifestyles of the Rock and Roll world were not enough to convince you that their style of music is wicked, then let us examine the words and themes of the songs themselves.

Ozzy Osbourne - Suicide Solution
Blizzard of Ozz - 1980

Wine is fine, but whiskey's quicker
Suicide is slow with liqueur
Take a bottle, drown your sorrows
Then it floods away tomorrows
Away tomorrows

Evil thoughts and evil doings
Cold, alone you hang in ruins
Thought that you'd escape the reaper
You can't escape the master keeper

AC/DC - TNT
TNT - 1975

I'm dirty, mean and mighty unclean
I'm a wanted man
Public enemy number one
Understand

So lock up your daughter
Lock up your wife
Lock up your back door
And run for your life
The man is back in town
So don't you mess me 'round

Guns N Roses - Used to Love Her
G N' R Lies - 1988

I used to love her
But I had to kill her
I used to love her, Mm, yeah
But I had to kill her
I had to put her six feet under
And I can still hear her complain
I used to love her, Oh, yeah
But I had to kill her
I used to love her, Oh, yeah
But I had to kill her

These are just three of literally thousands of examples of how Rock and Roll is filled with immoral, wicked, and sinful lyrics and themes. There are multitudes of songs that are so vile that I would never even put them in this book. There is no end to the godless debauchery of this industry! If you could imagine the most lewd and evil thing that can be done in this life, then I guarantee that there has been a Rock and Roll song written about that very thing! This entire industry is wicked to the core!

When faced with these facts, the only appropriate response for a Christian is to REPENT of any associations with this wicked industry. Rock and Roll is not good music that was hijacked by wicked men, but rather Rock and Roll is wicked music that hijacks good men to make them wicked. This musical style has the power to influence men to live as wickedly as possible. Rock and Roll is the musical manifestation of rebellion against God.

The major argument that those in the Christian rock industry make is that they are just taking the music

71

and changing the words to a more meaningful religious message. The truth that these people will never understand is that Rock and Roll is not bad words sung to good music, but rather the bad words are the vocal equivalent to the music itself. Rock and Roll is putting immorality to music. If the wickedness of a man's heart could be put in a song, that song would be Rock and Roll. Rock is sin. Rock is drugs. Rock is drinking. Rock is fighting. Rock is killing. Rock is death.

The logical fallacy is that these well-meaning people try to "Christianize" the words of the music of sin. They try to reach sinners with sin. This will never work! The great theme of the New Testament is that the Lord redeems sinful men and uses them for his glory! When a person trusts Christ as Savior, they are fundamentally CHANGED and are no longer the same (2 Corinthians 5:17). It is only when this drastic change occurs that God can use this person. Herein lies the major issue of "Christian" Rock and Roll: They try to convert something to God without changing it. To convert music to be used for the Lord means that it must be fundamentally changed from sin to God.

The clearest illustration that I can give to show you how ridiculous it is to take Rock and Roll and call it Christian would be for me to try to sell cocaine on the streets legally by calling it Christian Cocaine. Simply adding the word Christian before an illegal and dangerous substance does not make it legal and beneficial to one's health. To sell Christian Cocaine is just as much a logical fallacy as making a Christian Rock album.

ARE THESE SONGS

"CHRISTIAN"?

Christian: of, relating to, or professing Christianity or its teachings.

We often determine what type of music a song is by examining it's content. We know a love song by its content, a country song by its content, and a fight song by its content. If a song is to fall under the category of "Christian," then we must agree that there must be some mention of Christ, God, Calvary, Heaven, the Bible, Church, or a litany of exclusively Christian doctrines and concepts. (Examples of this would be: assurance of salvation, the blood of Jesus, the comfort of the Holy Spirit, Christian service, peace in your heart from knowing Christ, etc.) We should also consider that when love is mentioned in a song it should be specifically the love of God. If we do not do this, then we will have to say that songs like Whitney Houston's "I Will Always Love You" are Christian. We simply cannot do this and be intellectually honest.

When dealing with this subject, we must raise the question: What if a musician came out with a supposedly "Christian" album and he/she did not mention ANY of the aforementioned concepts? Could we classify this album as "Christian" and be intellectually honest? This has happened many times. Let us examine a few examples.

"Go West Young Man" - Micheal W. Smith
Go West Young Man - 1990

I'm blazing a trail that leads to vice
So easily enticed
By darker means
When out of the wilderness of choice
I hear that one small voice
Call to me

Go West young man;
Go West young man;
When the evil go East
Go West young man;
Go West young man;
Find a heart that's golden.

Why must I wander like a cloud
Following the crowd.
Well, I don't know,
But I'm asking for the will to fight,
To wear the Crown of Life
And You say go.

The mind is weak, the heart is frail,
When it goes beyond the pale
So unwise...

"Place In This World" - M.W. Smith
Go West Young Man - 1990

The wind is moving
But I am standing still
A life of pages
Waiting to be filled
A heart that's hopeful
A head that's full of dreams
But this becoming
Is harder than it seems
Feels like I'm
Looking for a reason
Roamin' through the night to find
My place in this world
My place in this world
Not a lot to lean on
I need your light to help me find
My place in this world
My place in this world

A careful examination of these lyrics will reveal that there is no direct mention of any major scriptural theme in these songs. The first song mentions the "Crown of Life" in such a vague and erroneous way that there is no way that we could connect it to a Bible truth. The second song uses the phrase, "I need your light to help me find my place in this world." How do we know that this is a prayer to God or a friend asking to use a flashlight? This is just another use of vague language that is meant to appear "Christian" without being so.

"Live it Well" - Switchfoot
Where the Light Shines Through - 2016
(This song was #6 on the Christian Top 40 Hits
chart as of September 2016)

I wanna sing with all my heart a lifelong song,
Even if some notes come out right and some come
out wrong,
'Cause I can't take none of that through the door,
Yeah, I'm living for more than just a funeral
I wanna burn brighter than the dawn,

Life is short; I wanna live it well.
One life, one story to tell.
Life is short; I wanna live it well;
And you're the one I'm living for
Awaken all my soul.
Every breath that you take is a miracle.

Life is short; I wanna live it well, yeah
I got one life and one love.
I got one voice, but maybe that's enough,
'Cause with one heartbeat and two hands to give
I got one shot and one life to live.
One life to live, yeah,
And every breath you take is a miracle.

This song was quite popular when it came out, and
I'm sure that much money was made by the
production and distribution of this track, but I want
you to notice that the same pattern of vague lyrics
continues with this song. Is there anything in these
words that distinctively identifies it as a "Christian"
song? I would suggest that after looking at these
words it would seem plausible that a Muslim could

be singing this to his god. After all, it does use the phrase, "I wanna burn brighter than the dawn". Having known several Muslims, I do not say this sarcastically.

"Love With Your Life" - Hollyn
July 2016
(This song was #12 on the Christian Top 40 Hits chart as of September 2016)

There's only so much you can say
Til' words turn into noise.
Yeah we go round and round again
But people we were meant to blaze
A life that's beautiful
Yeah we got so much love to give

Don't look to the left or right,
You know the future's worth the fight,
Don't look to the left or right
Hey, yeah,
L-O-V-E rolls off the tongue
But sometimes the word's just not enough,
Gotta dig a little, dig a little deeper.

You gotta love with your life
Like a fire burning strong;
Til' the night has come and gone,
There's a hope that lives in you
You gotta love with your life.

This is another great example of vague lyrics in a supposed "Christian" song. The only evidence that this song is Christian is the usage of the phrase, "There's a hope that lives in you." This is not enough to classify it as a Christian song because it is just a vague mention of a Bible phrase. If we are going to classify a song as "Christian" because it uses a phrase found in the Bible one time, then we must call ALL songs that use phrases like, "broken heart," "cast the first stone," or "for everything there is a season" as Christian songs as well. These common phrases do not make a song "Christian."

In my opinion, the one band that is the epitome of what is wrong about "Christian" rock is a band called "Devil Wears Prada". I first learned of them by working with some teenagers that attended a Church of God Church in East Tennessee. They shared with me a love for this band and spoke as if they were the spiritual giants of this generation. I found it odd that the way they spoke of these people was exactly the same way that the lost world spoke of their rock stars. "They are amazing!" "They totally rock!" "I met those guys and they are so cool!" Immediately a red flag went up in my spirit about this group. I went online and watched several music videos produced by this band and was shocked at what I saw! This band was NO DIFFERENT than the rock and metal bands that I had listened to as a lost, heathen teenager. Let us examine the words to one of their most popular songs.

"Born To Lose" - Devil Wears Prada
Dead Throne - 2011

You don't know what you need.
We're all so back and forth,
Nothing is as it seems.
You don't know what you need.

We make the same mistakes,
We've ruined everything.
What is it this time?
What must you call holy?
This is your lifeline,
Nothing is at it seems.
If I were you I'd give it up.
If I were you I'd care.
I'm born to lose
With a noose around my neck.
World be gone and move forward.
I abhor you,
With every selfish thing that you say.
None of it is the worth the time.
You don't know what you need.
We're all so back and forth,
Nothing is as it seems.
You don't know what you need.
We make the same mistakes,
We've ruined everything.
Born to lose
With a noose around my neck

An honest observation would conclude that there is nothing in this song that could legitimately classify it as a "Christian" song. Many of those who like this song would say, "This song uses the word HOLY! That makes it a Christian song, right?" My answer would be an emphatic NO. If the mere mention of words like: holy, love, and hope constituted a "Christian" song, then we must conclude that the most popular "Christian" musicians of all time have to be Dolly Parton, Whitney Huston, Celine Dion, and Justin Beiber; we know that is not the case. We must also realize that the mere mention of these sayings does not classify a song as "Christian" either. If the mentioning of phrases like "power of God," "eternity," "light," "Christ," "disciples," "Heaven," "angel," "Lord," "Jesus," and "the cross" made a band "Christian," then we would have to conclude that the most Christian band in the world is Slayer; we know this isn't the case. For a song to be legitimately "Christian" it must be sound in doctrine, message, and style.

In 2013, Maria Godoy of NPR radio published a disturbing article about the contents of McDonald's beloved Chicken Nuggets. They found that the contents of these nuggets were not 100% chicken, but rather fat, ground bone, and nerves.

"Chicken nuggets: Call 'em tasty, call 'em crunchy, call 'em quick and convenient. But maybe you shouldn't call them "chicken." So, say Dr Richard deShazo a Professor of Pediatrics and medicine at the University of Mississippi Medical Center. In a research note published in The American Journal of Medicine, deShazo and his colleagues report on a small test they conducted to find out just what's inside that finger food particularly beloved by children. **Their conclusion?** "Our sampling shows that some commercially available chicken nuggets are actually fat nuggets," he tells The Salt. "Their name is a misnomer," he and his colleagues write. "The nuggets they looked at were only 50 percent meat — at best. The rest? Fat, blood vessels, nerve, connective tissue and ground bone — the latter, by the way, is stuff that usually ends up in dog food." [26]

What McDonald's does is take a small amount of

true chicken meat and combine it with what is essentially "filler" material, add chicken flavoring, bread it, fry it, and serve it to the public. The final product is advertised as "Chicken" McNuggets, when ultimately there is very little actual chicken meat to be found.

This same tactic is used by the "Christian" Rock Industry. They take a TINY amount of Bible truth, add the "filler" of Rock music, dance routines, smoke, mirrors, top notch graphic design, stylish musicians, tours, radio ads, trendy clothes, laser shows, fry it in the oil of "positive thinking," and serve it to the masses as "Christianity." Once you realize that the Churches of America have been on a steady diet of this since the 1960's then you may realize why so many Churches are "out of shape."

The basic truth of this chapter is simply this: the vast majority of "Christian" Rock music is NOT Christian in doctrine, substance, or musical style. It is simply a misleading, marketing tactic used to create another genre of music so that the record companies can sell more albums (1 Timothy 6:10).

Let us now examine some popular songs in the realm of what is commonly referred to as "Traditional Hymns". These traditional hymns have been commonly used in hymnals among most denominations in America and England. In this chapter, we will post the lyrics of these songs and identify the major Christian doctrines that are mentioned.

81

Amazing Grace

Amazing grace! (Grace of God) How sweet the
sound
That saved a wretch like me! (Salvation)
I once was lost, but now am found; (Salvation)
Was blind, but now I see. (Salvation)
'Twas grace that taught my heart to fear, (Grace of
God)
And grace my fears relieved; (Grace of God)
How precious did that grace appear (Grace of God)
The hour I first believed! (Salvation)

The songs documented earlier in this chapter
are not even worthy to be compared to the amount
of depth and meaning that can be found in this
classic Christian anthem.

Rock of Ages

Rock of Ages, cleft for me, (Death of Christ for Sin)
Let me hide myself in Thee; (Salvation)
Let the water and the blood,
From Thy wounded side which flowed, (Death of
Christ for Sin)
Be of sin the double cure;
Save from wrath and make me pure. (Salvation)
Not the labor of my hands
Can fulfill Thy law's demands; (Sinfulness of Man)
Could my zeal no respite know,
Could my tears forever flow,
All for sin could not atone;
Thou must save, and Thou alone. (Salvation)

How could anyone question the depth of meaning

and rich insights that the author of this song had of Christianity. This song is dripping with precious Bible truth! How can we even say that Michael W. Smith was a Christian musician when his songs show little to no evidence of Christian doctrine? Especially when compared to these classic songs.

If you are reading this and disagree with what I am saying, I want you to realize that even Michael W. Smith agrees with me.

In an interview with Larry King in 2014, Michael W Smith was asked to describe his music. Read the transcript below:

KING: So, is it (Smith's Music) described as gospel? Is that a fair description of what you sing... What do you say it is?

SMITH: You know what I just think **it's pop music, you know.**" [27]

I rest my case. Selah.

ARE THESE MUSICIANS EVEN

CHRISTIANS?

In an earlier chapter, I told the story of how I visited a "Christian Rock" concert in my hometown. I called the Church and asked if I could interview the bands at the concert. The youth pastor of the church graciously agreed to allow me to do so.

I called a friend and asked him to come and be my camera man while I interviewed these musicians. Once the first band in the concert finished playing, we found them at their table signing autographs and handing out CDs. I politely approached them and asked them if they would like to do an interview on camera with us. They graciously agreed and we walked outside because the noise in the gym was so overpowering.

When we set up for the interview I asked them a very simple question: "When did you get saved?"

The lead singer of the band began to give me an erroneous story about how he was "raised around it and I had a bunch of different things that I got into and I kinda got out of it; and then it was like a year and a half ago, I was like, you know like, I wasn't like doing heroin or anything, but I was like, smoking pot and stuff; and I had a drug test I had to take at school and like, there was no way I was gonna pass it; and I prayed and said, 'Oh God would you get me out of this and I'll do whatever?' I passed the drug test and I decided that I needed to stop being retarded."

This was so strange to me because I was hoping that he would give me something that sounded like a testimony of salvation, but it was nothing of the sort. When I asked him about his conversion all he could tell me was about him asking God to help him pass a drug test, but nothing about him asking God to save him from Hell. I was really bothered by this! Could it be that this guy was a well-meaning religious man, but not saved?

The next band that I interviewed had a lead guitarist named Kevin. He was gracious enough to allow me to interview him on camera. I asked Kevin when he became a Christian.

His response was, "I became a Christian when.........my first Christian experience was when I was 5. It was one of the most phenomenal experiences of my life. Coming from my background there was a lot of violence and hatred in my life. It was just nice to get around people that could be compassionate and love me for me. And so, just a phenomenal experience; just like a week at camp completely changed my life."

I paused after his response and asked him the same question again: "When did you become a Christian?"

His response was: "I'm a big guy and people like to test big guys and I got into fights a lot. So, you know, just all the violence was just consuming my life. All this hatred, I would just hate everything and these people, you know, they would just love me and they didn't even know me. So, it kinda just threw me for a loop there. That's basically what did it."

I was so bothered by this strange non-answer that he gave me, that I decided to ask him a third time about his testimony. I simply asked him: "Can you pinpoint for me a time that you became a Christian?"

Kevin's response was: "A time?! Um..... Well...... Um..... Well, there was this time that they played this song at camp, and that was the first time that I had actually given my life to God. They played this song called "Fire Fall Down" and I just kinda stopped and stared at the floor and I thought, "You know, these people love me and they don't even know me." Nobody before had ever done this before. So, I started thinking that maybe this is what I need. Maybe this is the smack in the head that He gave me to wake me up and say "Hey! There are people here who love you and you don't have to hate everything. You don't have to hate anything." And...that's what did it for me. I just remember staring at that floor. I could point it out."

This was only the second interview I had done that day and I could easily see a trend was happening. These people had a testimony that had no mention of being born again. I was just hoping that it was a misunderstanding on my part. Sadly, this wasn't the case.

Adam and Shane from another band were the next people that graciously agreed to do an interview with me. I asked Adam how he became a Christian and his response was, "I became a Christian at a really young age I was actually brought up in Church so, you know, I was already familiar with it, but I didn't decide to get baptized or decide to fully become a Christian in the terms that I knew it until I was about 16. We started our band when we were young kids, like 12, and so we probably just started it so, you know, we could just play around and have fun and we discovered when we were older that we could use it for better things than just playing in our basement and just having fun. We found that we could actually get out and do some good work with it."

I honestly had no idea what he meant by "I got baptized and fully became a Christian." I was once again troubled by these strange answers that I was getting. The strangest answer came from Shane.

I asked Shane the same question I had asked all of them, "When did you become a Christian?"

Shane responded, "There was this teacher I had in high school that invited me out to his house just to eat dinner with him and get to know him. He kinda mentored me in some different ideas of Christianity that we more appeasing and more humanistic with what I knew. That is how I found my way with Christ."

I asked him again if there was a time and place that he could nail it down that he became a Christian. He responded, "Yeah, um, I was on a bike ride home. There was a trail that connected from the teacher's house to my home. I was just thinking how gracious and benevolent they were. I really felt like that was a lot like what Christ was doing when he was here. I felt really humbled by that and it blessed my heart."

What is going on here? Why are these guys in a full-time band unable to give me a clear testimony of their salvation? The only real honest conclusion is that they are religious but LOST. I understand the implications of this conclusion, but I also know that there are many scripture verses that demonstrate this same principle.

John R Rice wrote a booklet called, "Religious But Lost", in which he outlines many instances where people have a head knowledge of God, but have never truly been born again.

"Not every one that saith unto me, Lord, Lord, shall enter into the kingdom of heaven; but he that doeth the will of my Father which is in heaven. Many will say to me in that day, Lord, Lord, have we not prophesied in thy name? and in thy name have cast out devils? and in thy name done many wonderful works ? And then will I profess unto them, I never knew you, depart from me, ye that work iniquity." - Matthew 7:21-23.

"Multitudes of people who expect to go to Heaven will go to a Hell of torment. Thousands of "good" people, "moral" people, church members, even church workers - yes, and, alas, even prophets, priests and preachers - will find themselves lost when they expected to be saved, condemned when they expected approval, cast out of Heaven when they expected to be received into eternal bliss. That is the explicit meaning of the words of our Lord quoted above.

Newspaper columns sometimes carry stories of "Life's Most Embarrassing Moment," but nothing in life could ever bring the horrible humiliation, disappointment and blame that is here described and awaiting multitudes who think they are saved but actually lost. They claim salvation; they shall receive damnation. They are self-satisfied under a delusion, a false refuge; before Jesus Christ they will be horrified to hear that He never knew them.

Mark you, this is not a warning that people should beware lest they lose salvation. Jesus did not say He would turn against those He once knew, that He would reject those He once knew, that He would reject those He had once accepted. Rather, to multitudes of professing righteous people He solemnly warns that He will be compelled to say to them, 'I never knew you. You never were saved; you never were born again.'

Many of those who say, 'Lord, Lord,' will never enter the kingdom of Heaven. Many of those who have done wonderful deeds, even claiming to have done them in Jesus' name, will fail to be received into Heaven. They are professors without possession. They are church members, perhaps, but not Christians. They are reformed but not reborn. They have lamps but no oil. They are dwelling under the delusion that they are all right when really they have wicked hearts covered with sin and dwell under the wrath of Almighty God!" - John R. Rice, Religious But Lost

Could this be so? Could there really be multitudes of people that are religious but lost? After years of studying the Bible, I have to say that this is the sad case with mankind. MOST of mankind will be in Hell when they die.

We see this warning many times in the Scriptures. We see the Apostle Paul wrote "Examine yourselves, whether ye be in the faith; prove your own selves" (2 Corinthians 13:5). We see that the Apostle Peter wrote "Wherefore the rather, brethren, give diligence to make your calling and election sure" (2 Peter 1:10). We find that Isaiah spoke about people that had a false hope in eternity:

"Because ye have said, We have made a covenant with death, and with hell are we at agreement; when the overflowing scourge shall pass through, it shall pass through, it shall not come unto us: for we have made lies our refuge, and under falsehood have we hid ourselves: Therefore thus saith the Lord God, Behold, I lay in Zion for a foundation a stone, a tried stone, a precious corner stone, a sure foundation: he that believeth shall not make haste. Judgment also will I lay to the line, and righteousness to the plummet: and the hail shall sweep away the refuge of lies, and the waters shall overflow the hiding place. And your covenant with death shall be disannulled, and your agreement with hell shall not stand; when the overflowing scourge shall pass through, then ye shall be trodden down by it." Isaiah 28:15-18.

Friend, this is the great controversy of our day! Could it be that these people of the "Christian" Rock world are those who are like "whited sepulchres, which indeed appear beautiful outward, but are within full of dead *men's* bones, and of all uncleanness." (Matthew 23:27)? Could these multitudes of people be those that the Apostle Paul was referring to when he spoke of those that are "Having a form of godliness, but denying the power thereof:" (2 Timothy 3:5)? Could these people be those that Jude spoke about when he said, "Woe unto them! for they have gone in the way of Cain, and ran greedily after the error of Balaam for reward, and perished in the gainsaying of Core. These are spots in your feasts of charity, when they feast with you, feeding themselves without fear: clouds they are without water, carried about of winds; trees whose fruit withereth, without fruit, twice dead, plucked up by the roots; Raging waves of the sea, foaming out their own shame; wandering stars, to whom is reserved the blackness of darkness for ever." (Jude 11-13)

The implications of these verses are literally mind blowing, but they must be said. Maybe this entire book should not be about lost people trying to "Christianize" Rock and Roll, but rather that lost people try to be religious without being saved! Maybe the real issue here, is that these people try to "Christianize" Rock and Roll because they fundamentally misunderstand the nature of God. They do this because they do not know God. This really is nothing new. (Ecclesiastes 1:9)

Mankind has always tried to appease God, man's way rather than trying to appease God, God's way. These people have been spoiled by "vain deceit" (Colossians 2:8) and have spent their lives, "going about to establish their own righteousness, have not submitted themselves unto the righteousness of God." (Romans 10:3)

There are also many instances of well-known preachers, that have thought they were saved, when they truly were not. The best-known example of this has been John Wesley. Daniel Walther, Professor of Church History, Potomac University, wrote an article called, "Conversion Experiences of Great Leaders," for Ministry Magazine in April of 1959.

"At the age of thirty-two he decided to embark on a mission to the Indians of Georgia. If we are to believe Wesley himself, his main purpose in going to America was 'the hope of saving his own soul.' And the obvious question was asked, 'Do you have to go to Georgia to save your soul? Can't you do that just as well in England?' He answered, 'No, neither can I hope to obtain the same degree of holiness here which I may there.' He does not indicate the reasons that made him think that the climate of Georgia and his contact with the Indians would be more propitious to the saving of his own soul.

During these years of spiritual growth, he often came in contact with the Moravians who seemed to point the way and give him spiritual counsel. Thus, on the shores of Georgia he was greeted by a Moravian pastor, Augustus Spangenberg, who asked him bluntly: 'Does the Spirit of God bear witness with your spirit that you are a child of God?' To this question Wesley had no answer to give. Again, he was asked, 'Do you know Jesus Christ?' Then he paused and said, 'I know that He is the Saviour of the world.' 'That is true,' said the Moravian, 'but do you know He has saved you?' 'I hope He has died to save me,' replied Wesley.

The well-educated Oxford divine was thus given a rather rude reception on coming to America, but it revealed that he was unaware of the basic spiritual condition of his own life. He admitted that he knew the way of salvation, but not the experience. There was little in his early sermons about Jesus as the Redeemer. Wesley stressed especially church formalism, strict formality, ceremonies, and ethics.

After a stay of a little more than two years in America, he returned to England. Again, he analyzed himself severely and found that after his experience in America, where he ostensibly went to save his own soul, he thought he had failed:

'It is now two years and almost four months since I left my native country in order to teach the Georgian Indians the nature of Christianity, but what have I learned in the meantime? Why am I, who went to America to convert others, not converted to God?' As is the case in Augustine's Confessiones and in any self-portrait, a man's words should be read with a certain amount of caution. To this last sentence, questioning whether he was converted, more than thirty years later he added the words, "I am not sure of this!"

And then the great moment came. The date: Wednesday, May 24, 1738. 'I think it was about 5:00 this morning that I opened my Testament upon these words, 'There are given to us great and exceeding promises, even that ye should be partakers of the divine nature.' Just as I went out I opened it again upon these words, 'Thou art not far from the kingdom of God.' In the afternoon, I was asked to go to St.

Paul's. The anthem was, 'Out of the Deep Have I Called Unto Thee, O Lord, Hear My Voice.' In the evening, I went very unwillingly to a society on Aldersgate Street where one was reading Luther's Preface to the Epistle to the Romans. About a quarter before nine while he was describing the change whereby God works on the heart through faith in Christ, I felt my heart strangely warmed. I felt I did trust in Christ alone for salvation; and the assurance was given me that He had taken away my sins, even mine, and He saved me from the law of sin and death." [29]

We must conclude that the concept of religious people who think they are serving God, but are not truly converted is a biblical concept and is true in Christian history as well.

Are you sure that you are saved (Ephesians 2:8-9)? Have you ever been born of the Spirit of God (John 3:7)?

𝕸INISTRY OR INDUSTRY?

The Webster's 1828 Dictionary defines "Ministry" as: "Ecclesiastical function; agency or service of a minister of the gospel or clergyman in the modern church, or of priests, apostles and evangelists in the ancient." (Acts 1:17, Romans 12:7, 2 Timothy 4:5, Numbers 4:12)

The definition for "Industry" is: "a particular form or branch of economic or commercial activity."

When dealing with the subject of "Christian" Rock we must define if this is a ministry or an industry. This will give us a vital insight into the motives of the people involved. If this is a ministry, then we must conclude that these people are simply misguided and well meaning. If this is an industry, then we have every right to denounce these people as charlatans who are using the Lord, the Church, and God's people to make a living as third rate musicians. It is vital that we see the difference.

We can gain much insight into this by reading what people that are in the music industry have to say about Christian music. Michelle Williams was one of the three women to make up the group Destiny's Child in the early 2000's. Williams grew up in Rockford, IL and her family attended a Church of God in Christ Church.

During the height of popularity for Destiny's Child, the group temporarily split up to pursue solo projects. Billboard.com did an article on Williams in April of 2002 about her new gospel album.

"With Music World/Sony's release this week of 'Heart to Yours'", Destiny's Child member Michelle Williams hopes to strike a gospel chord with the gushing fan base of teens who have made the group R&B's reigning female superstars. 'There is a song for everyone of every age,' Williams says, of the inviting collection of tightly synchronized harmonies that span inspirational and contemporary urban gospel to hardcore traditional.

Album highlights include guest vocals from Mary Mary, who groove with Williams on the Mervyn Campbell-produced cut 'Glad to Be Here (So Glad)'; Men of Standard, who back her on the rousing 'You Cared for Me'; R&B crooner Carl Thomas, with whom she teamed for a remake of BeBe & CeCe Winans' classic 'Heaven'; and lead single 'Heard a Word.' Williams' duet with Shirley Caesar on the traditional 'Steal Away to Jesus' was previously featured on Caesar's Grammy Award-winning 'Hymns' album." [29]

The most revealing part of this is the last paragraph of the article. Williams makes a shocking revelation about the gospel music industry:

"Some people will do Gospel when their career fails, but I chose to do it at the height of the popularity of Destiny's Child," Williams explains. "And I didn't want to do it because it was a fad. I wanted to do it because it's in me. It's in my heart."

Williams makes the statement that Gospel music is a fallback for those failing in the music industry and a fad. This incredible revelation reveals that there are many people making Gospel music because they failed in the secular music industry.

Let us use the next paragraph to illustrate the reality of the situation. Let us say that the music industry is likened to Major League Baseball. You have the big leagues with the National League and the American League each comprised of several different teams. You also have a reserve of people that are in the Minor Leagues. These people are in reserve in case a slot comes open in the Major Leagues. Those in the Minor Leagues are constantly playing baseball and improving so that they can one day "hit it big" and get their shot at the Major League. Those who are in the Major League that do not perform well are eventually sent down to the Minor League until they can improve enough to play in the Major Leagues again.

This same analogy can be used with the secular music industry. The Major Leagues are Country, Rap, Pop, and Rock music. The Minor League is the Contemporary Christian Music INDUSTRY. These people are using Churches as platforms to build their fan base and their musical skills in the hopes of someday making it to the BIG LEAGUES!

This analogy has been tested and proven true in many cases. On one hand, there are some that legitimately want to share Christ with the world, they think that if they become famous as a musician, then they can have that opportunity; on the other hand, there are those who are spiritually warped people that will do whatever they have to do to become famous, including pretending to be a Christian band.

There are also those that have made huge amount of money in the music industry whose careers have become stagnant. They have not made a hit album in years and the opportunities to perform for large crowds has dwindled. These people do a "gospel" album in an effort to revitalize their careers. Musicians that have done this are Randy Travis, Bob Dylan, Little Richard, M.C. Hammer, and Ma$e.

There are numerous examples of people that started singing in churches as musicians only long enough to build a fan base and then made it to the "Big Leagues" as secular musicians. People like Whitney Houston, Usher, Katy Perry, Jessica Simpson, Diana Ross, R. Kelly, John Legend, Aretha Franklin, Avril Lavigne, Faith Evans, Brandy, Carrie Underwood, Joy Williams (of The Civil Wars), Mutemath, Sixpence None The Richer, Amy Grant, Faith Hill, and even Third Day has done this.

Yes, even Third Day has done this exact same thing. They sold out and it will only get worse because this is how this entire industry works.

In October of 2014, rollingstone.com did an article called, "Third Day Singer Mac Powell Continues Country Cred With New Album 'Southpaw".

"Two years ago, I made my first country record and a lot of people thought, 'He's got it out of his system now," Powell tells Rolling Stone Country, "but all that did was make me want to do it even more.

And thus was born Southpaw, the singer's follow up to his 2012 self-titled country debut. The 12-song set, released October 14th, includes co-writing with country hitmakers Darius Rucker, Kristian Bush, and Travis Tritt. It's arguably a natural transition for the bearded, long-haired Alabama native with a penchant for musical storytelling. Yet certainly not a permanent one. In his other life, the father of five is one of the most awarded artists in Christian rock music. For more than two decades, he's been the lead vocalist and principal songwriter of the Christian band Third Day. The band has won four Grammys, 24 Gospel Music Association Dove Awards and are members of the Georgia Music Hall of Fame. Third Day is still together; Powell is just continuing to pursue what's been a longtime career goal.

I grew up listening to country music, says the musician, whose family moved from Clanton, Alabama, to Atlanta when he was a teen. 'I'm from the south, so you're surrounded by it whether you like it or not; but fortunately I do like it a lot, and I always have. I've wanted to do country music for a long time. I put it off for many years because of time and fears, all sorts of different reasons, but I finally got to a point where I couldn't put it off any longer. I was already looking back going, 'Man I wish I had done this five years ago." [30]

Mac Powell claims that he only did this country album because he has always been around country music, but I will tell you without hesitation that Mac Powell did this album for money and fame. If you

101

were a pitcher in the minor leagues barely making a living and got a call from the Atlanta Braves to start pitching for them, would you turn down the offer? What else would make a man sing about Jesus rising from the dead on one album and mocking his own sin on the next album?

Well Sunday Morning I go to Church
I say my prayers and read the Word
Tryin' to find forgiveness for what I did Saturday
- Mac Powell, "Saturday"

Mac Powell is a sad case that will only get worse in time. Unless he does a spiritual 180° he will continue down the path of money and carnality and he will eventually become exclusively country. I will also suggest, that in time, Casting Crowns will do the same thing. We shall see...

In June of 2016, christianpost.com put out an article called, "Puff Daddy Taps Gospel Singers to Join Bad Boy Reunion Tour".

"Puff Daddy's Bad Boy reunion tour is doing more than bringing some of the biggest names in 90s Hip Hop back together, with the music mogul inviting gospel musicians on the tour as well.

Isaac Carree, age 43, and Zacardi Cortez, age 30, are singing background vocals on the Bad Boy Family Reunion Tour that reunites entertainers Puff Daddy, Lil Kim, Ma$e, Faith Evans, Mario Winans, Total, Carl Thomas, 112, and The Lox in venues around the country.

Carree has taken to Instagram to repost messages about his 13-hour tour rehearsals with fellow background singers Andrea "Latrelle" Simmons, who has written for the likes of Destiny's Child and Monica, fellow singer-songwriter Keisha Renee, and fellow gospel musician Cortez.

Cortez went on to repost an Instagram video of him singing about Jesus, which was posted by songwriter LaShawn Daniels.

"Everything We Do We Bring The POWER Of The HolyGhost," Daniels wrote before tagging Cortez's Instagram page. "@cardikee #ChurchBoyz #Trusted #BadBoy20Years #badboyreunion."

It may come as no surprise to some that Puff decided to tap into gospel music influences on his tour. The record executive and recording artist spoke about using the concert to glorify God.

"I give all glory to God for this opportunity to come and see all of our true BADBOY FANS LIVE AND IN CONCERT! I want to thank all of you that have supported us over the last 20 years," he wrote in an Instagram message reposted by Cortez. "It's truly been a journey and a blessing! God is the GREATEST!"" [31]

Just so that there is no misunderstanding, this article is saying that Sean Combs (Puff Daddy) recruits people out of the "Christian" gospel rap and pop industry so that they can sing on the Bad Boys Tour about fornication, drugs, drinking, breaking the law, fighting, and using every cuss word known to the

English vocabulary. Gospel artists could be singing "Amazing Grace" one week and doing backup vocals for Jay-Z as he raps to his wicked songs the next week. This is unbelievable!

"Out of the same mouth proceedeth blessing and cursing. My brethren, these things ought not so to be. Doth a fountain send forth at the same place sweet water and bitter?Can the fig tree, my brethren, bear olive berries? either a vine, figs? so can no fountain both yield salt water and fresh." - James 3:10-12

Being that "the love of money is the root of all evil" (1 Timothy 6:10), should we really be surprised when someone who is not deeply devoted to Christ would sell out for the fame and fortune of mainstream musical success?

Another tactic that is used by many businesses is called "finding your niche." This tactic teaches that a group must search and discover what people are in the market for and create a product that fills that "niche." If people are wanting music that makes them angry, then they produce angry music. If people want music that makes them emotional, then they create a product that does that. In an earlier chapter, we discussed the concept of the "Sinner-Saint" culture that America has now embraced. This has created the "niche" in the music industry where people want to listen to hard rock (Sinner) with religious lyrics (Saint).

The great example of this has been a group called Switchfoot. Switchfoot has experienced much mainstream success because they seem to be enjoyed by those who want to hear Rock music and those who want to hear Religious music. They have been very open about it. In June of 2006, Dave Tianen of the Milwaukee Journal Sentinel interviewed Jon Foreman of Switchfoot about their music:

"We've always been very open and honest about where the songs are coming from. For us, these songs are for everyone. Calling us 'Christian rock' tends to be a box that closes some people out and excludes them, and that's not what we're trying to do. Music has always opened my mind — and that's what we want'.

Yet in many ways they used the opportunity to describe their split from the CCM industry. This has caused some, such as Spin writer Andrew Beaujon, to take the view that 'their lyrics often have two different meanings, one meaning for a Christian audience and one meaning for the rest of us. They try to relate to two different groups of people at once." [32]

This article accurately describes what this group is trying to do. They are trying to be both secular and sacred, both lost and found, both rock and gospel. Just like Elvis Presley...

Why do this? The answer for all of this is simple: Carnality. You simply cannot be "vexed with the filthy conversation of the wicked" (2 Peter 2:7) in the music industry and expect to be able to "walk in the light, as He is in the light, we have fellowship one with another" (1 John 1:7) at the same time. There is a dividing line that God Himself has drawn.

"Wherefore come out from among them, and be ye separate, saith the Lord, and touch not the unclean thing; and I will receive you, And will be a Father unto you, and ye shall be my sons and daughters, saith the Lord Almighty." - 2 Corinthians 6:17-18

The World Agrees With Me

In my research of this subject, I was truly surprised to find that many prominent secular people agreed with me on this subject. They see the error of trying to merge the Church with the World and they resent it more than I do. In this chapter, I will give a few examples.

Billy Connoly

In 2011, Comedy Central released a DVD of Billy Connoly's comedy sketch: You Asked For It. During this comedy special Connoly began to rant about Christian Rock and Rock. "Christians should not be allowed anywhere near Rock and Roll," he said, "It's not for them!" He also called Christian Rock and Roll an "absurdity."

South Park

During my research, someone pointed out to me that South Park did an entire episode on the subject of "Christian" Rock and Roll. I was given a transcript of the episode and the basic plot was that the kids of the show place a bet on who could get a platinum album first. Cartman decided to pursue a "Christian" Rock band while the rest of the boys decide to pursue a traditional Rock and Roll band.

As I read the lines of the opening scene of the episode, I was SHOCKED at what they said! The entire scene is basically the thesis of the book that you are now reading!

Cartman: "Think about it! It's the easiest, dumbest music in the world! If we just play music about how much we love Jesus, all the Christians will buy our music!"

Kyle: "That's a dumb idea Cartman!"

Cartman: "It worked for Creed!"

Stan: "I don't want to be in a stupid "Christian" Rock band!"

Cartman: "You just start that way and then you cross over! It's Genius!"

It was also pointed out to me that later in the episode that Cartman was quoted as saying, "Alright guys, this is going to be so easy! All we have to do to make Christian songs is take regular old songs and add Jesus stuff to them. See all we have to do to make Christian songs is mark out works like 'baby' and 'darling' and add words like 'Jesus".

I find it sad that even the world sees through the hypocrisy of those that try to marry wickedness and holiness together for a profit, but American "Christianity" does not.

Levi Lowrey

Levi Lowrey is a personal friend of mine. Having grown up in the same town together, we have known each other for a long time. Levi was always talented in music and was expected to make a living as a musician. Levi began writing country music and has been very successful in his short career.

"He was nominated for a CMA Award for Song of the Year, and won a BMI Country Award for Top 50 Songs of the Year, both for "Colder Weather," the No. 1 hit he co-wrote with frequent collaborator Zac Brown. Lowrey and Brown also co-wrote "The Wind," from the Zac Brown Band's No. 1 Billboard album Uncaged, as well as the rollicking "Day For The Dead," from the newest ZBB album, The Grohl Sessions Vol. 1.

As a performer, he has received numerous accolades, as well, being singled as one of its "13 For 13: Ones To Watch in 2013 -The New Artists," as well as having his debut album honored as its third-best country album of the year in 2011-both by Roughstock.com.

True to his reputation as a talented writer, Lowrey penned four of the 14 songs on the self-titled album alone, and co-wrote the other ten. Each brings a brutal honesty that offers insights into different parts of Lowrey's life. He's a happily married father of two with a successful career who helps his wife homeschool his children whenever he can, but he's not afraid to explore subjects that others might find too uncomfortable for casual conversations." [33]

In my research of Levi's career, I found one particular song that he wrote that peaked my interest. "Before the Hymnal Died" is a reflection of Lowrey's childhood growing up in a Southern Baptist Church in Dacula, Georgia.

"I wrote this song...I just got nostalgic about singing hymns in the Baptist Church growing up. I try to go back every once in a while, to the contemporary services or whatever. I used to be a worship leader so I can speak out against them. I just can't get behind it. It really drives me crazy. I just don't think that the world needs songs about dancing through the fields of daises with Jesus. Just to be honest. I've always been a fan of the hymnal; flipping through the pages and realize that is where God meets you there. I also saw this t-shirt that said, "Save The Hymnal"....So I wrote this song." [34]

- Levi Lowrey, Live at Eddie Owen Presents at Red Clay Theatre in Duluth, Georgia. May 31, 2013

Before the Hymnal Died

"I grew up in a Baptist Church,
Back before the hymnal died
Everyone knew everyone.
You were sitting in the countryside.

Pretty soon you would come of age;
It was time to join the Choir.

110

That's where I learned Harmony;
Back before the hymnal died.

This describes me I know what you mean;
The assurance never seemed so sweet.
I'm near the cross and I am thine;
Back before the hymnal died.

I flipped through the pages but my eyes grow tired;
Dog eared pages and a broken spine.
Now we watch a screen and their ain't no choir;
Disregarded from a former time.

The church I know just what you meant,
The cross is rugged and its old and bent;
And I sang about it when I was a child,
Back before the hymnal died.

Now I try my best to go to church;
I smoke cigarettes til the worship starts.
But my boys will never know the words,
Of the eloquent lyrics sang to God's own son."

I find it amazing that this country song writer has
more spiritual discernment about music than many
in the "Christian" Rock and Roll world. He sees the
shallowness of lyrics and he laments the fact that his
kids will never know the songs that he knew growing
up. If these "Rock and Roll" churches do not wake
up and realize the direction they are going is not
right, then we will lose the blessings of God upon our
country.

EXIT STRATEGY

When one begins a small business, it is important that you make the right decisions early on, and many financial advisors say that an essential element for a business plan is something called and "exit strategy". An exit strategy is a plan to get the money that a business owner has invested back out of the business. This way there is minimal loses if the business fails. In this chapter, I am going to give you an exit strategy if you are wrapped up in the "Christian" Rock and Roll movement so that there is minimal loss to your life and spirituality. I would hate for you to waste your life in something sinful.

1. Know that You Are Saved

There was a day in my life where I loved Rock and Roll, Rap, Techno, and Heavy Metal music. I would go everywhere with that hypnotic beat in the background. I loved it and thought that I could not live without it. I feel that I was literally addicted to it!

When I was 18 years old, a soul winner from the Peachtree Road Baptist Church gave me the Gospel. He told me that in order for me to go to Heaven, I had to be born again. He then quoted John 3:7, "Marvel not that I said unto thee, Ye must be born again." I immediately expressed to this man that I did not know what that meant or how to be "born again." He shared with me Romans 10:13, "For whosoever shall call upon the name of the Lord shall be saved."

I fell under what old time preachers used to call, "Holy Ghost Conviction." I was troubled by what this man was telling me. I felt that the Holy Ghost was drawing me unto himself. That night, I got on my knees and asked Jesus Christ to save me from Hell. When I stood up I felt different immediately. I became a new creature (2 Corinthians 5:17)! My attitude, demeanor, clothes, actions, friends, places I went, and outlook on life completely changed! I was different!

When I got saved, the Spirit of God moved into my heart and began to change me. One of the main things that the Spirit of God changed was my taste in music. I would listen to my old Rock and Roll and the Spirit of God would reprove me. It was almost as if the Lord was saying, "You don't need that anymore." Instead of listening to secular Rock and Roll, I would try to listen to "Christian" Rock and Roll. The Spirit of God spoke to me and convinced me that there was no such thing as "Christian" Rock and Roll.

I find that many that are in the "Christian" Rock and Roll industry are not truly saved. Are you trusting Christ for your salvation? Has there ever been a change in your life? Has Christ made you a new creature? If you died today do you know for sure that you would go to Heaven?

2. Realize That You Are Wrong About Music.

The ones that claim that God is using "Christian" Rock and Roll are on the wrong side of Christian history. There is no other way than to simply say that they are wrong. Rock and Roll is fleshly and those who would say that it is not, are simply lying. This book has examined those who are in the "Christian" Rock Industry and those in the secular Rock Industry and we have found that they behave basically the same. Cussing, anger, hate, bitterness, and immorality are commonplace in both of these groups.

"Now the works of the flesh are manifest, which are these; Adultery, fornication, uncleanness, lasciviousness, Idolatry, witchcraft, hatred, variance, emulations, wrath, strife, seditions, heresies, Envyings, murders, drunkenness, revellings, and such like: of the which I tell you before, as I have also told you in time past, that they which do such things shall not inherit the kingdom of God." - Galatians 5:19-21

Maybe these groups act the same because they are the same?

3. Ask the Lord to Lead You to a Bible Preaching Church.

A church? Yes, the reason that you are weak spiritually is because you are either in the wrong kind of church or not in church at all. Find a Independent Baptist Church that preaches and teaches from the King James Bible, and uses the right kind of music. You may be surprised to see that many churches like this exist!

Conclusion

Despite the many personal attacks that may occur as a result of writing this book, I know that this is what the Lord wanted me to do. I am not a mean-spirited person that finds fault with everything and everybody. I am a happy Christian that loves the Lord, my life, and my family.

I wrote this book, not because I am on a crusade against a certain type of music, but because I am genuinely burdened for many people out there that are just like me when I was a lost teenager. I thought that I was a Christian, but I was never truly born again. There are so many in this world that are reformed but not reborn. I find many of these people are in the "Christian" Rock and Roll world.

I beg with you to trust Christ!

"But as many as received him, to them gave he power to become the sons of God, even to them that believe on his name:" - John 1:12

MY PERSONAL TESTIMONY

I grew up in a small town in Georgia called Dacula. I never knew anything about the Bible or God. I went 18 years of my life without having one person witness to me about my soul. I knew many people who claimed to be a Christian, but they did not live any different than anyone else, so I thought that there was no need for me to become a Christian. When I was a senior in high school, I went half a day to one high school and half a day to another high school. One day, as the bus driver was driving two other students and I from one school to another, she turned around and asked us if we were saved. The two other students replied: "Yes, of course we are saved!" I replied: "I don't know if I am saved." At that very moment, I came under conviction of my sinful nature and knew that I had never been saved. I had heard other people talking about being saved and I had always wondered what being saved meant. I wonder if this woman had taken the Bible and showed me how to be saved, would I have gotten saved right there on the bus?

The thought of being saved or lost haunted me and I went months of my life under deep conviction of my sinfulness. I remember one time I was in my room with a close friend of mine and I asked him if he was a Christian. He lied and said: "Of course I am!", I replied by saying, "I wish that I could stop living this wicked life and become a Christian."

On my own, I tried many things to make me feel better about my sinful life. No matter what I tried to do to live better, I could never quit sinning. It was like the only thing that I could do was sin against God. I needed something to happen to me so that I could quit my sinful living. I knew that if I kept up my sinful life, that I would go to Hell when I died and I did not want that at all. I was under such conviction that I went to the local grocery store and bought a book called The Bible Promise Book. It was a book full of King James Bible verses that was sorted by topic. I bought the book, went home, and opened it to the Salvation chapter. Immedietely a verse jumped out to me and pierced my soul as an arrow.

"Verily, verily, I say unto thee, Except a man be born again, he cannot see the kingdom of God." John 3:3

This verse convicted me because I knew that whatever being born again meant, I was not born again. The book also gave the verse Romans 3:23.

"For all have sinned, and come short of the glory of God." Romans 3:23

As I read that verse I knew that I had sinned and come short of the Glory of God. I knew that I was a sinner and that all I was doing was sinning against God every day. This book also gave the verse Romans 6:23.

"For the wages of sin is death; but the gift of God is eternal life through Jesus Christ our Lord." Romans 6:23

As I read this verse I understood that there was a payment for my sin and that payment was death. The last thing in the world that I wanted to do was to die in my sin. I noticed the end of the verse, where it said that the Gift of God is eternal life through Jesus Christ our Lord; I wondered what having "eternal life" meant? Was that the same thing as "being saved"? As I read further into this book, it gave this verse in 2 Peter 3:9.

"The Lord is not slack concerning his promise, as some men count slackness; but is longsuffering to us-ward, not willing that any should perish, but that all should come to repentance." 2 Peter 3:9

As I read that, I knew that I did not want to perish (go to Hell). I understood that in order not to perish I had to come to repentance. I wanted to be saved, but I did like most people do, I waited to be saved. I went many more months of my life under conviction of my sinful life. In the fall of 2001, I had the opportunity to coach my brother's little league football team. One of the men that also coached was named Tim Prosen. Tim was a member of the Peachtree Road Baptist Church in Suwanee, Georgia. One day Tim invited me to come to Church on a Monday night and play a game of flag football. I was glad to be invited, so I showed up that Monday night. The date was November 5th, 2001. As we played the game, I noticed these people were not living the painful life that I was. I could see peace and joy in their faces. I did not know what these people had but I wanted it!

After the game was over, one of the men came up to me and asked me a strange question. He asked me: "Spencer, if you died today would you go to Heaven?" It seemed like, as those words came out of his mouth, a ton of bricks hit me right in the chest. I learned later that the feeling I had was called Holy Ghost Conviction. I was so overcome that I just stood there speechless. The man knew that I was under conviction. It was then that I started to walk back to my car to leave, but the funny thing is that I had parked on the other side of the church graveyard. So, as I started walking through that graveyard another man approached me. He said: "Spencer, I noticed that you did not answer that question a minute ago. If you were to die tonight would you go to Heaven?" I looked at the ground and said: "No…no I would not."

He looked me in the face and said: "Spencer, the most important thing that you could know in this world is that when you die you are going to Heaven." He said a few other kind words to me and encouraged me to come to church on Sunday before he went home. I felt God dealing with me about getting saved. It was then that I walked about 5 steps in that graveyard and fell on my face before God and asked God to save me from my sin and take me to Heaven when I die. I got up off the ground with peace in my heart! I felt like a giant load had been lifted off of me! I was BORN AGAIN! That next Sunday I attended church and have not missed a Sunday service since!

My friend, let me ask you a question: Have you ever been born again? There are many names for salvation in the Bible: saved, born again, having everlasting life. Whatever you choose to call it is fine, but if you have never been saved, then you will not go to Heaven when you die, you will be in the Lake of Fire. The Bible says in Revelation 21:8:

"But the fearful, and unbelieving, and the abominable, and murderers, and whoremongers, and sorcerers, and idolaters, and all liars, shall have their part in the lake which burneth with fire and brimstone: which is the second death." Revelation 21:8

"And I saw a great white throne, and him that sat on it, from whose face the earth and the heaven fled away; and there was found no place for them. And I saw the dead, small and great, stand before God; and the books were opened: and another book was opened, which is the book of life: and the dead were judged out of those things which were written in the books, according to their works. And the sea gave up the dead which were in it; and death and hell delivered up the dead which were in them: and they were judged every man according to their works. And death and hell were cast into the lake of fire. This is the second death. And whosoever was not found written in the book of life was cast into the lake of fire." Revelation 20:11-15

If you have never been born again, then you will be in the Lake of Fire when you die. Please, don't die in your sin and go to the lake of fire.

"For whosoever shall call upon the name of the Lord shall be saved." Romans 10:13

Simply put, if you will personally ask Jesus Christ to forgive your sin and give you His gift of eternal life, He will!Why don't you make this simple decision right now?

Call on the Lord now..."Lord Jesus, I know that I am a sinner, and that I deserve eternal punishment in Hell. I ask you to forgive me of my sin and to save me. I accept your gift of eternal life. Thank you for saving me from Hell. Thank you for the gift of eternal life,   Amen."

If you prayed that simple prayer and you believe that The Lord saved you, then we want to rejoice with you. Welcome to the family of God!

124

BIBLIOGRAPHY

CALLING EVIL GOOD
SPENCER SMITH

- 1. Odle, C. (n.d.). African American Religion in Early America. Retrieved October 07, 2017, from https://www.thefreedomtrail.org/educational-resources/article-religion.shtml
- 2. History of Rock . (n.d.). Retrieved October 07, 2017, from https://www.history-of-rock.com/freed.htm
- 3. Christian rock. (2017, October 07). Retrieved October 07, 2017, from http://en.wikipedia.org/wiki/Christian_rock
- 4. Biography. (n.d.). Retrieved October 07, 2017, from http://larrynormanlyrics.com/bio.htm
- 5. McFadden, M. (1972). *The Jesus revolution*. New York (osv.): Harper & Row.
- 6. Larry Norman. (n.d.). Retrieved October 07, 2017, from http://everything2.com/title/Larry Norman
- 7. Why Should The Devil Have All The Good Music Documentary (Full Movie). (2015, February 07). Retrieved October 07, 2017, from https://www.youtube.com/watch?v=3yHSJVSbe tM
- 8. -Larry Norman, "Why Should the Devil Have All the Good Music?", Linear Notes, *Rebel Poet,*

Jukebox Balladeer: The Anthology (September 2007).

- 9. Page 3 of Larry Norman: The Growth Of The Christian Music Industry - Larry Norman. (n.d.). Retrieved October 07, 2017, from http://www.crossrhythms.co.uk/articles/music/ Larry_Nor- an__The_Growth_Of_The_Christian_Music_Ind ustry/24341/p3/
- 10. Stryper. (2017, October 05). Retrieved October 07, 2017, from https://en.wikipedia.org/wiki/Stryper
- 11. (n.d.). Retrieved October 07, 2017, from http://www.classicrockrevisited.com/show_inte rview.php?id=1028
- 12. Features | Dr Rock | To Hell With The Devil: Stryper Interviewed. (n.d.). Retrieved October 07, 2017, from http://thequietus.com/articles/03912-stryper- interview-michael-sweet
- 13. Bassist TIM GAINES Would Work With STRYPER Again As Long As 'God' Was Orchestrating It Read more at http://www.blabbermouth.net/news/bassist- tim-gaines-would-work-with-stryper-again-as- long-as-god-was-orchestrating- it.html#QRS1h0rFsH8mA8ly.99. (n.d.). Retrieved October 7, 2017, from http://www.blabbermouth.net/news/bassist- tim-gaines-would-work-with-stryper-again-as- long-as-god-was-orchestrating-it/#
- 14. Amy Grant. (2017, October 07). Retrieved October 07, 2017, from https://en.wikipedia.org/wiki/Amy_Grant

- 15. (1991, April 22). *USA Today*. Retrieved October 7, 2017.
- 16. (1991, July 15). *People*. Retrieved October 7, 2017.
- 17. James Chute, professional music critic for the Milwaukee Journal
- 18. Grant, T. (2014, August 05). The Great Decline: 60 years of religion in one graph. Retrieved October 07, 2017, from http://tobingrant.religionnews.com/2014/01/2 7/great-decline-religion-united-states-one-graph/#sthash.kbNLrmKe.dpuf
- 19. Chaves, Mark. 2011. The Decline of American Religion? (ARDA Guiding Paper Series). State College, PA: The Association of Religion Data Archives at The Pennsylvania State University, from http://www.thearda.com/rrh/papers/guidingpa pers.asp.
- 20. (n.d.). Retrieved October 07, 2017, from http://www.users.globalnet.co.uk/~wdhay/blac kbeat.htm
- 21. Chapman, M. W. (2014, December 31). Retrieved October 7, 2017, from cbsnews.com
- 22. Alice Cooper, Christian: 'The World Belongs to Satan'. (2014, December 31). Retrieved October 07, 2017, from http://www.cnsnews.com/blog/michael-w-chapman/alice-cooper-christian-world-belongs-satan
- 23. Kingkade, T. (2017, July 17). Remember All The Gross Accusations Against R. Kelly? Retrieved October 07, 2017, from http://www.huffingtonpost.com/entry/r-kelly-

sex-abuse-
allegations_us_56797582e4b06fa6887eb270
- 24. Christian rock. (2017, October 07).
  Retrieved October 07, 2017, from
  http://en.wikipedia.org/wiki/Christian_rock
- 25. Tame, D. (1988). *The secret power of music.*
  Wellingborough, Northamptonshire: Aquarian
  Press.
- 26. Godoy, M. (2013, October 11). What's In
  That Chicken Nugget? Maybe You Don't Want
  To Know. Retrieved October 07, 2017, from
  http://www.npr.org/sections/thesalt/2013/10/
  11/232106472/what-s-in-that-chicken-nugget-
  you-really-don-t-want-to-know
- 27. Michael W. Smith & Larry King, "Interview
  With the Kesse Family; Interview With Michael
  W. Smith," Feb 10, 2006, retrieved Dec 6, 2014,
  [transcripts.cnn.com/TRANSCRIPTS/0602/10/lkl.
  01.html] (*Emphasis mine)
- 28. Conversion Experiences of Great Leaders.
  (n.d.). Retrieved October 07, 2017, from
  https://www.ministrymagazine.org/archive/195
  9/04/conversion-experiences-of-great-leaders
- 29. Michelle Williams: The Destiny's Child
  singer sings about the Heart Of The Matter -
  Destiny's Child. (n.d.). Retrieved October 07,
  2017, from
  http://www.crossrhythms.co.uk/articles/music/
  Michelle_Williams_The_Destinys_Child_singer_
  sings_about_the_Heart_Of_The_Matter/39159
  /p1/
- 30. Price, D. E. (2014, October 22). Third Day
  Singer Defends Country Crossover. Retrieved
  October 07, 2017, from

http://www.rollingstone.com/music/features/
mac-powell-country-album-southpaw-
20141022

- 31. Christine Thomasos , Christian Post
  Reporter | Jun 3, 2016 9:15 AM. (n.d.). Puff
  Daddy Taps Gospel Singers to Join Bad Boy
  Reunion Tour. Retrieved October 07, 2017, from
  http://www.christianpost.com/news/puff-
  daddy-taps-gospel-singers-to-join-bad-boy-
  reunion-tour-164782/#xkofES97E3rt0xE5.99
- 32. Http://www.journalinteractive.com, J. I.
  (n.d.). Retrieved October 07, 2017, from
  https://web.archive.org/web/20060706140202
  /http://www.jsonline.com/story/index.aspx?id=
  444350
- 33. News. (n.d.). Retrieved October 07, 2017,
  from http://www.cmt.com/artists/levi-
  lowrey/biography/
- 34. G. (2013, June 01). Levi Lowrey "Before The
  Hymnal Died". Retrieved October 07, 2017,
  from
  https://www.youtube.com/watch?v=MEc30vgA
  uE8